Companion Gardening
in Australia

*Feel your garden with your heart and soul. Wonder
at its creation and at the inner beauty of its intricate
structure, its fine line of balance. Breathe in its peace
and vitality, and know you are fulfilling your role
as a keeper of the Earth.*

Other titles by this author

How to See and Read the Human Aura
Affirmations for Life

Companion Gardening
in Australia

WORKING WITH MOTHER NATURE

JudithCollins

 hachette
AUSTRALIA

DEDICATION

I wish to thank the thousands of people and all the groups who have
visited me at Earthkeepers, encouraging its development. You have
waited so patiently for this book and I, for my part, have made certain
that all you asked for is contained within. I also wish to thank the
members of the NSW Organic Growers' Association, the Permaculture
Society and the Natural Health Society of Australia for their support.
A special thank you to my father-in-law for starting me off on the
right foot and helping me realise a dream. And to my husband Paul—
friend and companion.

⌂ hachette
AUSTRALIA

Published in Australia and New Zealand in 2008
by Hachette Australia
(an imprint of Hachette Australia Pty Limited)
Level 17, 207 Kent Street, Sydney NSW 2000
www.hachette.com.au

Reprinted 2009

First published in 1993
by Thomas C Lothian. Pty Ltd

This new expanded edition published in 1997

Reprinted 1999, 2003, 2005

Copyright © Judith Louise Collins 1993, 1997

National Library of Australia
Cataloguing-in-Publication data:

Collins, Judith Louise

Companion Gardening in Australia

New ed.

ISBN 978 0 7336 2334 9

1. Companion Planting - Australia. 2. Gardening - Australia. I. Title

635.0994

Illustrations by Julia McLeish
Designed by Jo Waite
Typeset in Sabon by Jo Waite Design
Produced by Phoenix Offset
Printed in China

Hachette Australia's policy is to use papers that are natural, renewable and
recyclable products and made from wood grown in sustainable forests.
The logging and manufacturing processes are expected to conform to the
environmental regulations of the country of origin.

Contents

Introduction

I came to what seemed a Garden of Eden in rural Thirlmere, where every plant, flower, herb and animal is first given life and then allowed to develop as nature intended. This was Earthkeepers, where I found others like me basking in the soft autumn sunlight, soaking up the tranquil atmosphere of this unusual garden. There were groups, who had come like pilgrims from all over New South Wales.

Amber De Nardi, *Macarthur Advertiser*, June 1991

Earthkeepers, the place I call home, is described by numerous visitors as a place of great inspiration. A camera, notepad and pen quickly become vital tools in capturing it all, and all the gardens are signposted, detailing their usage and role so that the visitor may look and learn.

Earthkeepers has been a long time coming. I have been an organic gardener since my teens, and even at school I chose to work in the gardens rather than play sport. It was there I learnt to take cuttings and to add mulch and compost to the soil.

I remember vividly the teacher explaining how compost conditioned the soil and how there would be a noticeable change in the garden. Every day for a week, I went to see if the soil had changed. When nothing had happened I gave up looking, but I went back to the teacher with countless questions. From the answers I gained a basic understanding of gardening, on which I have built ever since.

My love of gardening at school did not extend to our garden at home, despite encouragement from my mother. While I was happy to bring her cuttings from school, I was reluctant to invest the same enthusiasm in her garden. I thought watering by hand was the most boring job ever created. Now I delight in it, finding it peaceful and relaxing.

In the first six months of my marriage we lived in a caravan. We cleared a little space beside it to grow a few plants to make it feel more homey. My mother donated a few geraniums and impatiens cuttings. Tying some string between two neighbouring trees, I planted beans among my flowers. They grew large, tasty and disease-free. Years later I learnt that the common white geranium is an insect repellent and a true friend to the bean family. On reflection, I laugh at my luck—or was it intuition?

My mother is an exceptionally practical person. When we moved into our first house, she bought me a general gardening book and a mattock for my birthday. Little did she know that this would be the beginning of bigger things to come. My brother Michael had dabbled in growing a few vegetables for one or two seasons. Apart from that, I had only been exposed to Mum's spring plantings of tomatoes, parsley and shallots—not forgetting the Derris Dust. I had no background in edible landscaping. This was to evolve through experience, and an inner connection to nature that I have always felt.

A tight budget meant looking for methods to cut costs: seed saving, cuttings, compost and mulch making, managing pests and disease. In the early years I observed my father-in-law, a country boy by birth, who is instinctively attuned to nature. Some say he has a green thumb. I know it to be more than this. I watched, listened, and learnt from him.

In search of the good life, my husband and I sold our house and bought a retired Estonian free-range chook farm that boasted a few stone-fruit and citrus trees. It was set in beautiful countryside at Thirlmere, near Picton. The property had been rented for some years with little nurturing. Fruit trees, camellias and bush roses had been pruned almost to rootstock with a chainsaw, to make way for grazing sheep.

There were lots of old sheds. In time, we sorted what could be saved from what would be toppled for scrap and recycling. Blackberries had taken hold. We cleared one area and found a horse cart. Surprises of this kind gave us the enthusiasm we needed to face the cuts and bruises, aches and pains.

Still looking for a change, I enrolled to study in Hawkesbury Agriculture College. It was there I found direction and a deepening of commitment.

Fellow students and several tutors showed great interest in what I had established and achieved on my property. The various organic and thermal gardens; the companion-planted orchard with its patrol of chooks, geese and ducks keeping pests at bay; the edible water gardens and the herb and cottage gardens. It was strongly suggested that I open the property to interested groups such as high school students, horticultural and agricultural students as well as gardening groups. I took this advice and provided part-time access to groups.

'Going public' meant that the property had to have a name. My husband, Paul, derived the name Earthkeepers from our deep belief that the Earth has been entrusted to the care of humankind. We felt that our garden should be an example to individuals of how to heal the environment. In learning about the ecological management of our landscape, we each become an Earthkeeper.

They say the best form of advertising is by word of mouth. In a matter of months I found the place besieged by people. There were new demands and they came directly from the public: open to everyone! I left work and opened the property on a regular basis. Conducted tours brought countless enquiries for a specialised course and access to specialist companion plants not commonly found in a general nursery.

Fifteen years of lecturing experience and community education in my previous career allowed me to transfer my teaching skill to a new subject with ease. It took little time to prepare an organic food growing course. It was welcomed with open arms, but people still hungered for more. In the months that followed I developed and taught more and more courses: Companion Planting, Growing and Using Herbs, Storing the Home-grown Harvest, Seed Saving and more. Perhaps my favourite course of all is Friendly Weeds, as they tell us so much about the health and well-being of the garden. A companion plant nursery was opened. It, too, flourished; but in the end, it was unfortunately not possible to continue the open access that gave so much delight. I was forced to close the gardens because of wear and tear.

Unauthorised plant cuttings devastated some of the plants.

The gardens needed time to recover so I decided to open only once or twice a year.

There is not a day goes by that I don't look around me and thank God for the opportunity to live a dream. The freshness, the smell of crisp air, the tranquillity and the connectedness to the Earth—creation itself. On entering the gate at Earthkeepers, visitors remark on the spontaneous sense of inner peace they feel and the special stillness which expands one's awareness. It's because the spirit of Mother Nature takes refuge here.

CHAPTER 1

Companion Planting

A philosophy to live by

Who are we? Mere specks upon the Earth? Beings in a long chain of inhabitants? Yet we believe we are supreme and all-knowing. It only takes a lightning strike, a flash flood or a hail storm to tell us otherwise. What controls can we expect to exercise over our environment when deep down we know we are not the controllers?

In the quest of humankind to prevent the crippling famines and disease of centuries past, much has been lost and the balance of nature ignored. High-yield food production has been achieved with single-plant crops (monoculture), but the degenerative effects on the land are only now apparent. Through ignorance and a lack of connectedness to nature we eradicate pests by the thousands, only to find they have been replaced by more persistent insects and diseases. In tackling our many problems we mostly offer ourselves convenient fixes, solutions for the short term only.

Companion planting offers the means to overcome our problems by restoring nature's balance to the environment. How many people know the value of the plants around them? When you see a dandelion in the lawn, is it a weed spoiling the perfection of your garden or a wild herb, creating a home and food for earthworms? If it is a wild herb, you have grasped the philosophy. Everything is interrelated, in harmony and balance. Everything is purposeful; in everything there is a lesson to be learnt. If you understand this, you are likely to succeed with companion planting.

Companion planting is not a seasonal occupation or hobby and it is more than planting garlic next to cabbages to ward off the cabbage worm. There are two approaches. Nature's way is a jungle of ground covers, flowers, shrubs, small and tall trees, everything in a natural order of its height, size, root system and need of light. It is encouraged to self-sow and manage itself. The controlled way is an ordered area displaying your taste in edible plants, perfumed flowers and shrubs, and handsome trees for colour and shade. I prefer nature's way, which respects a self-sown plant's ability to choose the most suitable place for it to grow.

I love to wander in my compact orchard because it resembles a woodland with surprises around every corner. I visit my feathered helpers. The geese prevent the grass from growing too high and interfering with the growth of the fruit trees, fruiting vines and companion plants. The ducks keep the area free of flies, snails and slugs. The chooks rotary hoe the floor of the orchard as they scratch for food. My helpers are also quick to eat fallen fruit, preventing grubs from harbouring in the soil. The jungle fowl roost in the fruit trees at night and disturb fruit bats who might be searching for a feast. I call my helpers 'the security patrol'.

If you are to succeed in companion planting your motivation is all-important. Are you seeking to control your garden or to manage it in a natural harmonious and ecological way? Remember, companion planting is about balance, not domination. We must learn to respect plants and let them work for us naturally. 'Primitive' cultures communicate with Mother Nature; they speak her language and read her signs, in rituals and in the management of their day-to-day life. We need to recover this ability.

When I see the weed amaranth in amongst my stone-fruit trees, I don't gasp with irritation and violently rip it out. I look at it for the clear message it is giving: the soil is good but needs aerating for the deeper roots of the trees. I let it do its job. Amaranth is a natural soil plough and can do a far better job than I. Once I had a clump grow up around a septic tank where the soil was cracked and soggy. Although the amaranth was unsightly, I decided to let it grow to maturity. Meanwhile, the geese burrowed a path through the clump and laid their eggs, no doubt seeking shelter from hawks who usually harass the chicks. When the amaranth matured, the soil was aerated and the chicks had grown big and strong enough to defend themselves. The amaranth became a useful ingredient for the compost bin. This large and cumbersome wild herb—weed—had provided a variety of services.

The following season, I noticed stinging nettle had replaced the amaranth. The next phase of soil improvement was in full swing. When it reached maturity it was slashed and left to lie on the ground to further service the area through its nutritional mulching properties. The next season I planted a nashi pear in the exact spot. For years I have watched it flourish free of disease—nature's doing, of course!

My experience has taught me that when plants are encouraged to grow naturally, weeds and all, they invite you to enjoy them instead of working for them.

Once I decided to let a corner of the garden return to its natural 'chaotic' state so as to stabilise itself. Several months later, on the approach of spring, I went to clear it for planting. To my amazement I found a perfect seven-kilogram cauliflower ready to pick. Its pearl-white head was the result of growing beneath taller plants; it had self-sown in a patch of weeds and been spirited along by stinging nettles and sow thistle. That evening the family ate the biggest and most delicious cauliflower casserole they had ever had.

I remember another time when a few onions had self-sown in a patch of weeds, wild carrot and sow thistle. They each grew to 800 grams and one weighed the even kilo. When I made up my mother's regular order of vegetables and fruit, I noticed that she asked for one large onion. For a laugh, I packed the kilo onion and I'll never forget the look on her face!

On a field trip to my property the members of the NSW Organic Growers' Association enticed me to pick a rhubarb leaf for them to photograph. The leaf stood 1.5 metres tall. I also remember the long intense stares from members of the Permaculture Society, as they attempted to analyse a nine-month-old producing brussels sprout plant which stood so tall that it had to lean against the kiwi fruit trellis to avoid snapping under its own weight.

Companion planting works for those who take the time and make the effort to know what they are doing. The results I have achieved are not unique. Believe in what you are doing and the garden will respond. Feel your garden with your heart and soul. Wonder at its creation and at the inner beauty of its intricate structure, its fine line of balance. When you have finished wondering, find a space where you can integrate your humanity, blending the spirit of yourself with the spirit of the garden, in pursuit of a harmonious relationship. In this, you will have succeeded in bringing about an ecological advancement in the garden. Place a comfortable garden seat in a cosy corner or somewhere with a tranquil view. Sit and ponder; feel the stillness of life in the garden. Breathe in its peace and vitality, and know you are fulfilling your role as a keeper of the Earth.

CHAPTER 2

Designing a Companion Garden

🐝 PLANNING

I have found that most people believe companion planting is about controlling insects with herbs. While they are on the right path, it is a narrow one. Many important functions of this natural ecological system have not been considered. Let's take a look at its role, holistically.

THE ROLE OF COMPANION PLANTING

- 🍓 The productivity of edible plants is increased
- 🍓 Essential oils and nutrients are increased
- 🍓 Destructive pests and diseases are reduced substantially
- 🍓 Diverse insects are attracted and provided with suitable habitats
- 🍓 Damaged plants are nursed back to health

- ❀ Plant and garden health is generally improved
- ❀ Soil is conditioned
- ❀ The garden is more attractive to earthworms
- ❀ On its maturity, the garden is self-governing
- ❀ The ecological balance of the world environment receives a small contribution
- ❀ A unique, natural beauty is fostered, emanating from the harmony of balance

The moment everything is in place, the garden begins functioning as a whole. Although the system is in its infancy, each plant is working towards fulfilling its role as an individual and as part of a co-operative.

Whether you are planning a mixed herb or cottage garden or an edible landscape, you need to do your homework so as to avoid costly mistakes, disappointment and repetitive labour.

There is a large body of information which will help you to formulate an appropriate plan and assist in the design of your garden. Most of the necessary information will be readily available. The remainder may take a little sleuthing on your part.

What you need to know

Let's have a look at what you need to know about your garden before designing its layout as well as selecting appropriate plants.

Favourite plants and their suitability to the local climate

You may like the taste or fragrance of a particular plant, but is it suitable for your climate? If not, it will be constantly stressed and battle to survive. Be sure to choose appropriate plants. Choosing the right plants for your climate will save you unnecessary expenditure and hard labour.

Maturing times, size and growth rate of plants

The placement of plants is made much easier when you are aware of the growing patterns of individual species. This information also helps if you are devising a plan for rotating your crops, which may be necessary for some vegetables, helping to avoid a build-up of disease in the soil.

Suitable indigenous edible plants

A number of these plants are helpful among fruit trees, as they attract fruit-eating birds and keep stone-fruit trees free from attack. Local birds mostly feed on local native plants—so plant some.

Weeds common to your local area

By gaining a knowledge of the weeds in your region, you will become aware of what is considered noxious and usually requires eradication. Some weeds attract harmful insects while others attract friendly predators.

Frequent and infrequent seasonal plant diseases

Knowing what diseases may be experienced by your garden will allow you to prepare to prevent them. Should they strike, you will know how to treat them.

The cycle of common pests

Each season has its own pests which you need to learn to identify by sight and by their behaviour. A garden can be prepared for the onslaught of pests. For instance, gardeners in areas prone to the Queensland fruit fly should plant trees that produce fruit either before the commencement of the fly cycle or after it has ceased. Some crops attract specific pests, and require a wide range of insect-repellent companions planted nearby.

Climatic conditions

Seasons don't automatically respond to dates on the calendar. You will find that expected temperatures may come early or late in your local area. In my area, spring temperatures can commence anything up to six weeks after the officially declared first day of spring. You should be aware of the length of your local growing period and when frost, snow, hail or heavy rain falls.

Soil testing

Plants will flourish or struggle depending on whether your soil adequately meets their needs. The soil type governs what you plant. From this knowledge you will gain an understanding of the needs of your soil.

Feral animals: friend or foe?

Areas that open onto bush or parkland often encounter feral animals. Knowing your friends and foes and the laws governing them will give you confidence in exercising your rights.

Supportive resources

There are numerous organisations that offer free advice from professional consultants. Some offer membership which includes continuing education, informative newsletters, seed exchange, specialist library facilities, educational field trips and more. There are also government advisory services offering free printed information and professional advice.

Speciality supplies

Locating a reputable herb nursery that carries a large variety of the plants listed in this book is essential, as is finding organic seed suppliers. Fortunately there are numerous mail order services nowadays.

Laws governing control of disease and pests

It is better to be safe than sorry. Ignorance is no plea for not meeting strict guidelines set to safeguard agriculture. At Earthkeepers we cannot bring ourselves to use chemicals, therefore we make certain that methods of natural management are in place. The fruit trees will not require spraying to combat fruit fly if they don't suffer from attack. Prevention is better than cure. For the past ten years our plum trees have never been infested.

When you have done your homework and compiled the necessary information, you are ready to design your garden the companion-planted way, with an organic emphasis.

🔺 Designing

When organic gardeners talk about design and companion planting, they are talking about the placement of plants, not just the shape and size of the garden. The design must be pleasing to the eye, while at the same time meeting the needs of the family and the surrounding environment. A pencil, a ruler, some drawing paper, an eraser and the reference listing in this book are the simple tools you require to become a creative environmental gardener. If you have done your homework, you should be clearly aware of plants suited to your locality, the condition of your soil, climatic demands, the types of disease and pests to guard against, and what it is you really want to grow, successfully.

The best place for designing a garden is at a table, not in the garden itself. I've heard numerous tales of woe from gardeners who purchased vegetable seedlings and a multitude of compatible herbs, then began to plant them out. Within moments, the companion-planting system became confusing and frustrating: plants everywhere, some without a home, others whose value to the garden had been all but forgotten. There are no short cuts in creating a companion-planted system. However, your efforts will give long-lasting rewards.

Guidelines for designing your garden

1   On a large piece of paper, draw a line to make two columns.

2   In one column list the flowers, vegetables, fruit, trees and so on that you wish to grow.

3   In the second column list their companions.

4 On another piece of paper, roughly sketch an outline of your garden plot. Indicate the position of north, south, east and west.

5 Mark the difference in areas, such as frosty, wet, open sun, partial or full shade.

6 Shade in the difference in soil types, for example clay, heavy or free-draining.

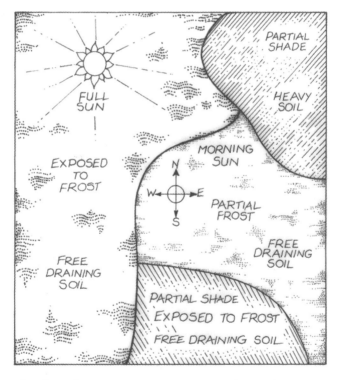

7 Sit back and examine your paper garden to locate suitable places to position plants so that conditions naturally encourage their growth.

8 Choose companions suitable for the space available in the garden.

9 Take a walk outdoors with your paper garden in hand and compare the plan and the actual garden site, making any alterations that may be necessary.

10 Gather your plants together and divide them into small groups pertaining to the planting zones outlined in your garden design.

You don't have to be a budding artist to sketch a garden plan and you don't have be a horticulturist to design a landscape. All you need to be is a lover of the world around you, with a desire for harmony and balance.

THE EDIBLE LANDSCAPE

Concern for their health and wellbeing is encouraging more and more people to make the most of every available space around the family home for the production of organic produce. Knowing where your food is coming from and guaranteeing its quality are the first steps to good health. The average house block is able not only to support the family which occupies it, but also to produce a surplus to share with neighbours from time to time. You don't need to plough your land or turn it into a farm paddock, nor does it have to be overrun with plants. All that is required is good planning, with an eye on current family needs. Is your swimming pool the focal point of summer living? Do you entertain mostly outdoors? Do you need a playing area for children? Do you need a fragrant glen in which to meditate daily? A landscape should service the needs and reflect the creative flow, attitude and lifestyle of its creators.

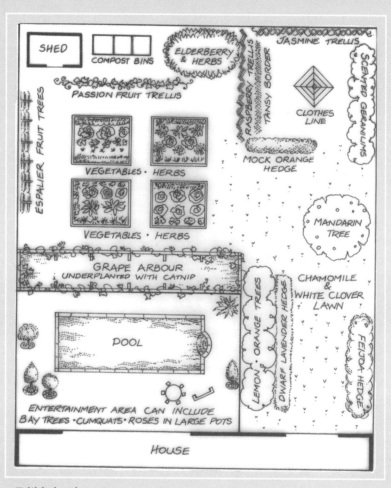

Edible landscaping

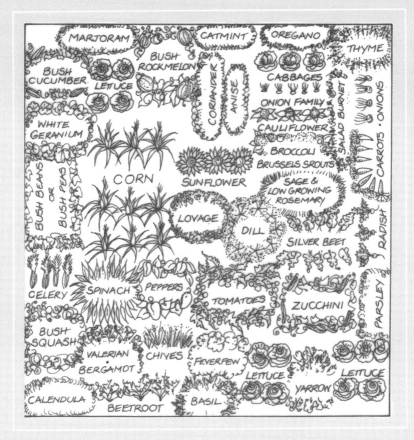

A companion-planted garden

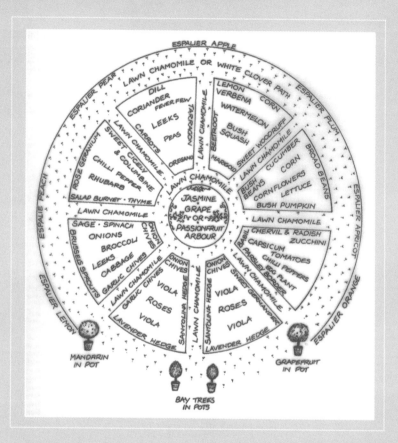

Herb garden

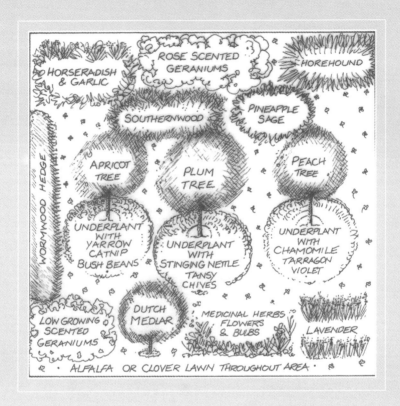

Stone-fruit trees

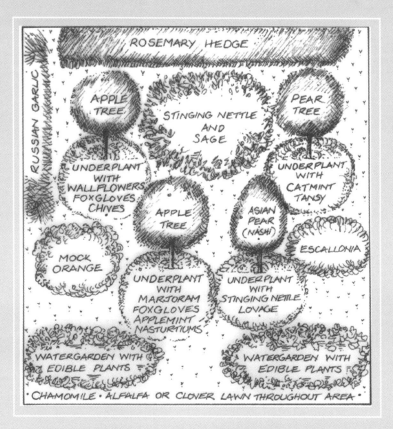

Inside the illustration:

ROSEMARY HEDGE

RUSSIAN GARLIC

APPLE TREE

STINGING NETTLE AND SAGE

PEAR TREE

UNDERPLANT WITH WALLFLOWERS FOXGLOVES CHIVES

APPLE TREE

UNDERPLANT WITH CATMINT TANSY

ASIAN PEAR (NASHI)

MOCK ORANGE

ESCALLONIA

UNDERPLANT WITH MARJORAM FOXGLOVES APPLEMINT NASTURTIUMS

UNDERPLANT WITH STINGING NETTLE LOVAGE

WATERGARDEN WITH EDIBLE PLANTS

WATERGARDEN WITH EDIBLE PLANTS

· CHAMOMILE · ALFALFA OR CLOVER LAWN THROUGHOUT AREA ·

Apple and pear trees

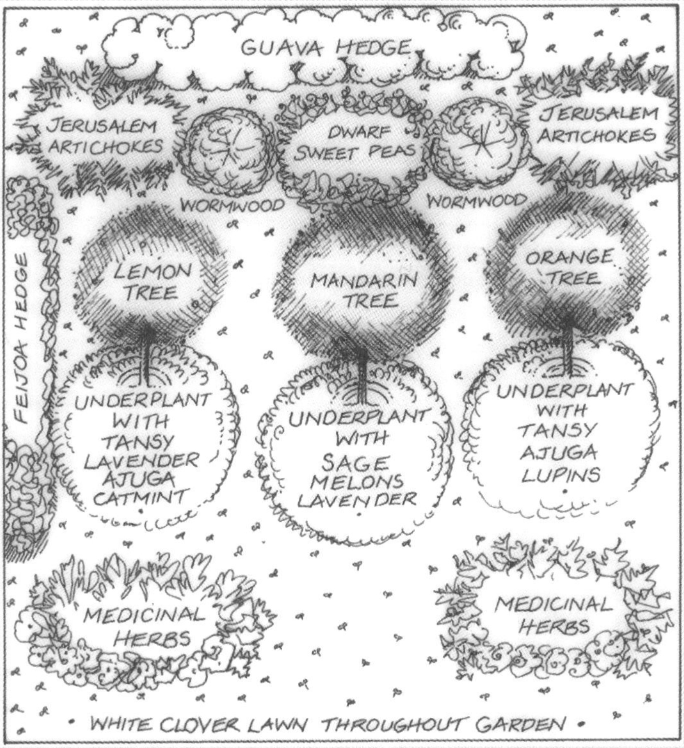
GUAVA HEDGE
JERUSALEM ARTICHOKES
DWARF SWEET PEAS
JERUSALEM ARTICHOKES
WORMWOOD
WORMWOOD
FEIJOA HEDGE
LEMON TREE
MANDARIN TREE
ORANGE TREE
UNDERPLANT WITH TANSY LAVENDER AJUGA CATMINT
UNDERPLANT WITH SAGE MELONS LAVENDER
UNDERPLANT WITH TANSY AJUGA LUPINS
MEDICINAL HERBS
MEDICINAL HERBS
WHITE CLOVER LAWN THROUGHOUT GARDEN

Citrus trees

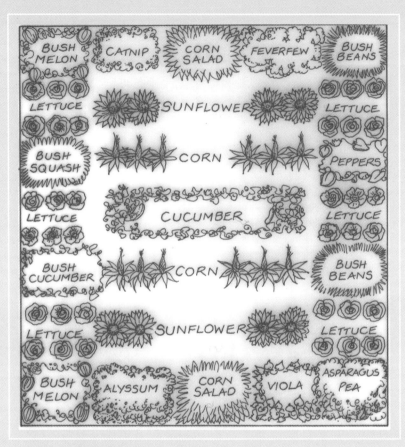

Corn and friends

Strawberries and friends

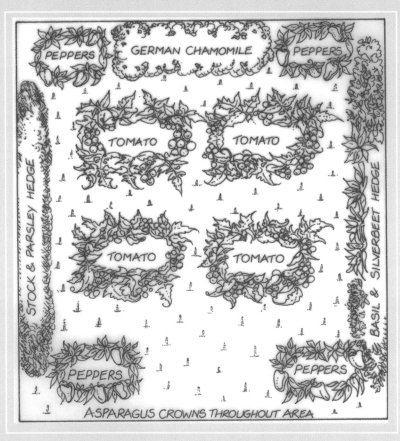

Tomatoes and friends

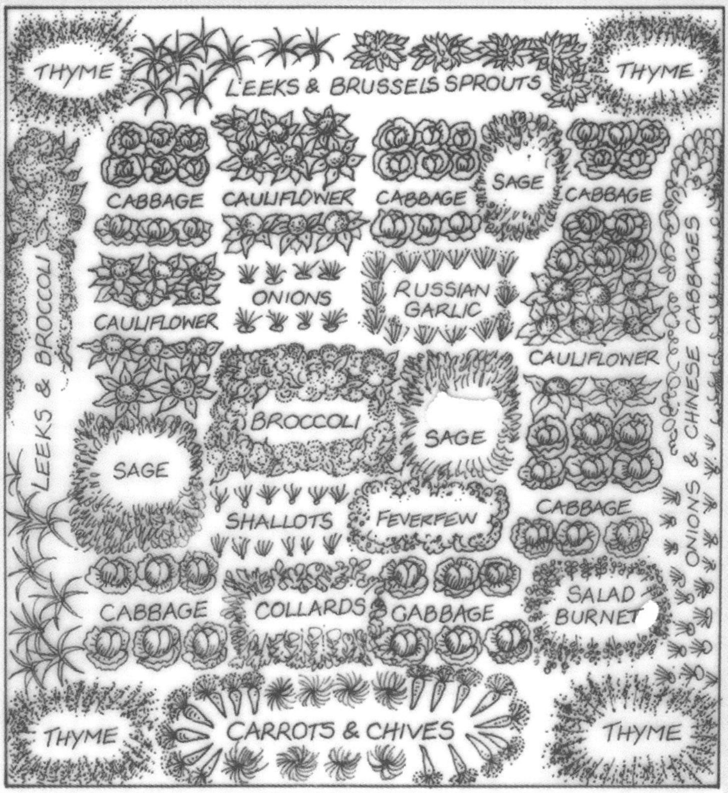
THYME
LEEKS & BRUSSELS SPROUTS
THYME
CABBAGE
CAULIFLOWER
CABBAGE
SAGE
CABBAGE
LEEKS & BROCCOLI
ONIONS & CHINESE CABBAGES
ONIONS
RUSSIAN GARLIC
CAULIFLOWER
CAULIFLOWER
BROCCOLI
SAGE
SAGE
SHALLOTS
FEVERFEW
CABBAGE
CABBAGE
COLLARDS
CABBAGE
SALAD BURNET
THYME
CARROTS & CHIVES
THYME

Cabbages and friends

An insect-deterrent garden

PHASES OF LEARNING

Instant learning

People expect to learn about companion planting overnight, believing it only to be a matter of good planning. There is some truth in this assumption, but it has taken me years to accumulate my working knowledge.

As I have already mentioned, you need to adopt an attitude which is attuned to nature. One that can automatically accommodate a damaged or failed crop, without causing you to go into a frenzy and lose your faith in companion planting.

There is also much to be gained from reading books based on the practical experience of the author, thus giving you instant knowledge for instant learning. Once again, doing your homework can save an awful lot of headaches and costly mistakes.

Trial and error

When you begin, success may come slowly. The garden environment may take the full cycle of the four seasons—one year—before it shows any sign of progress towards balance. Areas that have been damaged and scarred by erosion, exploitation or civilisation may take longer, as they need to recover and then adapt to their new lease of life.

If you keep in mind that you are a learner driver on an uncharted bush track, you will quickly realise that you need to do three things. First, take advice: listen, read and learn. Second, drive cautiously: observe everything in your path. Third, navigate: plan your garden. After one year you will have gained experience from each of the seasons and be ready to advance.

Monitoring the system

In order to work hand in hand with the natural forces of life, we must understand and track their regularity and irregularity. If it sounds complicated and too much like hard work, let me assure you it's not. It simply requires a stroll in the garden and observation.

The garden is exposed to elements that are constantly changing and reshaping the seasons. This in turn affects everything else—the cycle of pests, fruit and flower production, soil conditions and so on. One year, you may be almost free of insect problems. The following year, the garden may suffer a major invasion. It is vitally important to understand your garden and any areas which may be vulnerable if it rains or hails too long; if there is no rain for months; if all of the neighbourhood snails come to visit; if the Queensland fruit fly is in plague proportion—I think by now you have the picture.

To create a monitoring system, I advise buying a pocket diary. Whenever you notice a problem in the garden, write it on the appropriate date in the diary. Also record what action or treatment you have applied to overcome the problem. Through briefly recording the activities of the garden you can ensure that it has the skills and resources to cope.

My diaries span several years. Therefore I know that my local area has a regular cool to cold period that begins in March–April and lasts until September–October. Such information is vital when sowing vegetables, bulbs and flowers. Monitoring your garden will bring a wealth of helpful information and draw you closer to nature.

When companion planting doesn't seem to work

Neighbours

The finely tuned process of companion planting relies on the balance of the garden's environment. This includes neighbouring properties. Countless numbers of rifts have evolved from the conflicting beliefs of the organic gardener and his or her neighbours. Be wise, and encourage support. Enlighten your neighbours by offering produce, having short and effective conversations (no lectures) as well as sharing your expertise as you become more knowledgeable.

If your neighbours are treating their gardens with chemicals, expect your garden to entertain some of the neighbour's pests while it is learning to protect itself naturally through balance.

Seasons vary

Your garden may produce an excellent result one year, while the following year the outcome is less satisfactory. Don't immediately blame the garden. Perhaps there is a slight adjustment to be made in its design; or were there too many dry or wet spells? On review, were the temperatures in winter higher than average? Did a plague of pests descend on the neighbourhood?

There is always more than one reason for the system's poor performance. Should you continue to experience seasonal imbalances, the garden design may need rectifying to accommodate the garden's current needs.

An allopathic influence

Stunted plant growth makes this easy to detect. If you suspect one plant is inhibiting the growth of another, examine the situation carefully. When you are certain you have located the culprit, remove it, carefully making sure that no roots or seed pods have been left in the soil.

Too much competition

Plants require space to breathe and grow. Air must circulate around plants to avoid the development of fungal growths, rot and mildew. Check that plants are not competing for nutrients, sun and water.

Pest invasion

Have you planted companions which attract the same pest to the vegetable or fruit?

Rules for companion planting

There are a few simple rules that will lead you to success with the natural system of companion planting. Nothing need be complex if undertaken with commitment, enjoyment and a deep connection to your garden. Adhere to these basic rules to know all the rewards your garden can offer.

- **Understand your plants,** knowing each of them personally and understanding their individual needs— soil types, predators, diseases and so on.

- **Make appropriate plant selections** to support their needs and to provide them with adequate protection from pests and disease.

- **Allow plants to self-sow.** These plants tend to be less susceptible to pests and disease, reducing conflict in the garden. It is best to use non-hybrid seeds when making original sowings so that when the plant self-sows it will be true to the parent plant.

- **Learn to identify pests and predators** so that you are equipped to assist with the demands on your garden at all times.

- **Allow the garden to come of age** with the maturity of herbs. Herbs may need to be planted some weeks or months earlier than quick-growing vegetables and fruit.

- **Be a helper for Mother Nature** by permitting her to manage the garden. Work with her, not against her. Recognise the little signs she gives you, such as weeds.

✤ **Monitor the garden** regularly. Look for tell-tale signs of weakness in pest controls and in the design of the garden. Also look for climatic demands, like frost or sunburn. Identify the garden's strengths. Remember: difficulties are challenges which serve to strengthen our knowledge of ourselves and expand our skills.

✤ **Love your garden,** with all the devotion and respect it deserves. When you give love sincerely, you receive it twofold.

✤ **Remember you are a caretaker of the Earth** and have a duty to her well-being for the future of humankind and the millions of species who depend on us to behave responsibly.

CHAPTER 3

Companions for Life

ROLES OF COMPANION PLANTS

There are four methods by which plants help to bring an ecological balance to the garden. As you know, they come in all shapes, sizes, colours and odours, each contributing its own uniqueness. When designing and planning a companion-planted garden it is of vital importance that you understand the relationship between plants and how they will live and work together. As you become more and more familiar with companion plants you will notice that there are quite a few that are versatile in their role and in their behaviour. So you will not require a million varieties of plants in your garden—just a carefully selected complementary grouping.

It is necessary to understand the role of companion plants in order to gain insight into the strategies of a companion-planted system. By understanding the role of each plant you will come to recognise what it is doing for your garden. Plants help to bring an ecological balance to a garden in four ways:

Camouflage

Camouflage companion plants mask the scent of the plant that needs protection from destructive insects. The overpowering scent confuses the insects and encourages them to look elsewhere for food. The scents of tansy and fair Ellen geranium, for example, disguise the natural odour of tomatoes and kiwi fruit.

Plants:

> catnip, chamomile, eau-de-cologne mint, feverfew, geraniums (white and scented), sweet germander, lemon balm, the onion family, pennyroyal, peppermint, santolina, soapwort, spearmint, tansy.

Nurturing

Nurturing companions act as nurses, doctors and social workers in the plant world. They bring forth nutrients from the soil to improve plant health. They also help plants recover from disease or devastation by insect attack. In the company of nurturing companions, plants become strong and more resistant to disease.

Plants:

> sow thistle, marjoram, oregano, yarrow, valerian, lovage, stinging nettle.

Stimulation

Stimulating companions boost each other's essential oils, flavour, vitamins, minerals or productivity. It is this group of companions that permits the gardener to see and taste companion planting in action. Lettuce and strawberries grown in a patch of borage, for instance, abound with succulent flavour.

STIMULATING PLANT	STIMULATED PLANT
Borage	strawberries (juice, flavour and production)
Chervil	radish (makes it hotter)
Coriander	anise (germination of seed)
Elm tree	grapes (production and health)
Foxglove	neighbouring plants, especially apple trees
Garlic	roses (perfume)
Horehound	tomatoes (flavour)
Lovage	neighbouring plants (health)
Morning glory	melons (fruit production)
Mulberry	chokoes and grapes (fruit production)
Peppermint	chamomile (oil)
Rosemary	sage (flavour)

Salad burnet	mint and thyme (growth)
Santolina	roses (perfume)
Stinging nettle	peppermint (oil)
Tansy	orange tree (flavour of fruit)
Valerian	neighbouring plants (health)
Wallflower (perennial)	lavender (flower production)
Yarrow	aromatic and medicinal herbs

Sacrifice

Sacrificial plants are like lambs to the slaughter. This type of companion acts as a decoy, allowing itself to become smothered with pests, and at times totally infested, so as to protect neighbouring plants. Sacrificial companions are planted at a distance from plants that need protecting so that infestation does not spill over to them. For instance, I plant a large patch of yellow flowering nasturtiums at the far corner of the garden to attract all the aphids, thus giving plants in other parts of the garden a better chance of a healthy life.

Plants: horehound, nasturtiums, vegetables left to seed.

☙ Plant behaviour

Understanding how companion plants behave is important to the success of the system. It offers insight into how the garden is working. There are three types of behaviour:

Root secretions

Root secretions are nutrients transferred by companion plants through the soil and picked up by the roots of neighbouring plants. Companion plants need to be within root proximity of each other for this process to work effectively. Sow thistle brings nutrients up through the soil, allowing them to be tapped easily by shallow-rooted plants. Beans replace the nitrogen that corn leaches from the soil. Elderberry creates a rich humus within its drip line area that provides a healthy food source for companion plants.

Plants:

alfalfa, beans, borage, clover, elderberry, foxglove, horehound, horseradish, mustard, oleander, peas, rape, sow thistle, stinging nettle, yarrow.

Aroma

There are plants with aromas which attract beneficial insects and others which repel destructive insects and/or camouflage the scent of the garden. These plants work by releasing their essential oils into the atmosphere. The pungent leaves of the white geranium help to repel bean beetle. Lavender helps to repel borers in citrus trees. Some aromatic plants need no help from the gardener.

Plants:

> anise, candytuft, catnip, chamomile, curry bush, feverfew, white geranium, scented geraniums, hyacinths, lavender, lemon balm, marigolds, parsley, rosemary, rue, sage, santolina, tansy.

Other plants have difficulty naturally releasing their essential oils to the atmosphere and need to be bruised. A plant can be bruised in a number of ways: by a hard, sharp spray of water; by slapping or shaking it gently with your hands or by placing it in a raised garden bed or container in a windy passageway. The odour released when the tops of chives and garlic are cut will camouflage the smell of neighbouring plants.

Plants:

> chives (cut off the tops), garlic, mints, pennyroyal, southernwood, wormwood.

Dieback

For many herbs and weeds, dieback is a natural, seasonal process from which their perennial neighbours can benefit. The dead leaves of the companion may act as a mulch, or as a balanced plant food and health tonic. Some weeds and herbs rich in nutrients can be cut and left to wilt on the soil— stinging nettle is a perfect example. If you plant comfrey near roses its seasonal dieback process will strengthen them and help them to fend off rust.

Plants:

> bracken, comfrey, dandelion, elderberry, hazelnut, horsetail, melon vines, oak leaves, stinging nettle.

Don't be overwhelmed by the complex structure of nature and plant behaviour. Experience is a good teacher, showing you what is needed and directing you step by step to successful companion planting.

INSECT-REPELLENT PLANTS

A properly designed companion-planted garden should be antagonistic to a large range of destructive pests and be capable of deterring large numbers. In an invasion, insect-repellent plants will repel only 50–70% of the swarm. The shortfall relies on the health of the plant and beneficial insects. Non-hybrid seeds appear to be less susceptible to insect attack and to recover quickly. A healthy and balanced companion-planted garden is less likely to attract destructive insects and pests . The plants in this list can be expected to manage many of the demands placed on the garden from season to season. The remainder of problems will need to be treated with sprays, special plant food, compost or mulch.

INSECT	PLANT CONTROL
Ant	tansy, spearmint, pennyroyal
Aphid	red and orange nasturtiums, tobacco, chives
Aphid (woolly)	clover, chives
Bean beetle	white geranium, marigolds, potatoes, onions, turnips
Borer	tansy, lavender
Cabbage butterfly	peppermint, tomato
Carrot fly	parsley

Codling moth	common oleander
Cucumber beetle	radish, tansy
Flea	chamomile, lavender, santolina, fennel, fleabane, tansy
Grasshopper	larkspur, horehound
Harlequin bug	radish, turnips, onions
Japanese beetle	rue, garlic, larkspur
Leaf hopper	geraniums
Mosquito	lavender, santolina, fleabane, balm of Gilead
Moth	rosemary (dried), santolina
Nematode	marigolds, mustard, French lavender
Stink bug	radish, Jerusalem artichokes
Thrip	marigolds, tobacco, red and orange nasturtiums
Whitefly	rhubarb, red and orange nasturtiums, marigolds

ATTRACTING BENEFICIAL INSECTS

Nature provides her own natural controls. Here are some plants that will encourage beneficial insects into the garden, substantially reducing the plant-destroying insects and helping to balance the cycle of nature.

PLANT	INSECTS ATTRACTED
Amaranth	ground and bombardier beetles
Anise	wasps
Celery (in flower)	wasps
Chamomile	hoverflies, wasps
Chervil	hoverflies, beneficial wasps and other insects
Clover	ground beetles, parasites of woolly apple aphids
Dandelion	wasps
Hawthorn	diamondback moth parasites
Hyssop	hoverflies, wasps and other insects
Ivy	hoverflies, wasps
Marigold	hoverflies
Marguerite daisy (white)	wasps
Mint	hoverflies, wasps and many beneficial insects
Mustard	wide variety of parasites
Ragweed	parasites of oriental fruit moths and strawberry leaf bugs
Poinsettia flowers	hoverflies

Stinging nettle	many beneficial insects (a very useful plant)
Strawberry	oriental fruit moth parasites
Sunflower	lacewings, wasps
Tansy	ladybirds
Yarrow	ladybirds, wasps

PEST	BENEFICIAL INSECT
Aphid	lacewings, ladybirds, hoverfly larvae, larvae of chalcid and braconid wasps, mantids
Caterpillar	larvae of ichneumonid and braconid wasps, paper-nest wasps, mantids (also birds)
Mealy bug	larvae of ladybirds, lacewings, larvae of chalcid wasp
Mite	lacewings, hoverfly larvae
Lerp (psyllid)	lacewings
Scale insect	larvae of ichneumonid and braconid wasps, hoverfly larvae, lacewings
Scarab beetle	flower and cleptidae wasps
Slater	ground and bombardier beetles
Spider mite	hoverflies, lacewings
Stick insect	larvae of cleptidae wasps
Thrip	lacewings, ladybirds
Whitefly	lacewings, ladybirds

🐌 FRIENDLY WEEDS

When I speak of some weeds being friends to the organic gardener, people usually look at me with a puzzled expression. I can see their minds ticking over— 'What is this woman talking about?' Unfortunately, our culture no longer understands the necessity for the integration of all living things. Consequently, we are afflicted with an attitude of eradication: if it's in the way, knock it down or run it over; if it's invasive, hit it with a poisonous spray; if it's unsightly, rip it out. As weeds fit most of these descriptions they are destroyed without a chance to explain their role.

There are weeds, and then there are friendly weeds. Holistic organic gardeners usually have their favourites: stinging nettle, dandelion, chickweed and sow thistle. Weeds are often the pioneers in a garden, preparing the way for a community of plants to follow or indicating whether the soil is ready for them.

PLANT	SOIL CONDITION
Amaranth	healthy, aerated soil
Bracken	nitrogen deficiency
Chickweed	healthy, slightly acid soil, rich in copper, iron, manganese and potassium
Dandelion	presence or imminent arrival of earthworms
Dock	acid soil, rich in iron; a weak plant indicates poor soil

Fat hen	well-balanced soil
Horehound	dry soil
Inkweed	rich fertilised soil
Stinging nettle	indicates the soil is rich in nitrogen
Sorrel	thrives on neglect—damp, acid soil
Sow thistle	high nitrogen levels

The nutritional value of some weeds

Once upon a time humans lived on weeds because they were recognised as wild herbs, full of nutritious and healing properties. As civilisation progressed weeds, because of their persistent and often indestructible nature, became a nuisance in the more picturesque established garden. Consequently they began to lose their status. During food crises such as wars, however, people have had to exist on weeds. So, from time to time weeds become a helpful and life-saving resource for humankind. The strong and tangy flavour of weeds has now been replaced by sweetly flavoured vegetables, but some weeds are richer as a food source. For instance:

PLANT	NUTRITIONAL VALUE
Amaranth	three times more calcium content and more protein, phosphorus, iron and vitamin C than spinach
Burdock	sugar, tannin, iron, calcium, vitamins A, B, and C
Chickweed	mineral salts including potassium and calcium salts
Chicory	mineral salts, vitamins B, C, K and P
Dandelion	twice as much calcium and vitamin A, more phosphorus and as much iron as spinach
Dock	four times the carotene (vitamin A) content of carrots and twice the vitamin C of oranges

Evening primrose	potassium salts
Fat hen	high level of iron, protein, calcium and vitamins A, B1 and C
Ground ivy	high vitamin C content
Common mallow	vitamins A, B1, B2 and C
Mexican tea	rich supplies of protein, iron, calcium and vitamins A, B1, and C
Stinging nettle	high level of chlorophyll and proteins, vitamins A, C and D and minerals such as iron and phosphorus
Purslane	potassium salts, vitamin C
Shepherd's purse	rich source of vitamin C
Sow thistle	rich in vitamin C, calcium, copper, iron and potassium
Yarrow	volatile oil with azulene and achilleine, a glyco-alkaloid. It is so rich that when making compost, you add only one part of yarrow to every ten thousand parts of raw compost

Controlling weeds naturally

- Companion planting—thickly

- Grazing chooks, geese, sheep, goats, rabbits in a cage and so on

- Green manure crop (lupins, peas, mustard, buckwheat, broad beans) as thick as it will grow

- Interplanting heavy feeders and ramblers like pumpkins, tomatoes, herbs, choko, banana passionfruit, hops, wisteria, nasturtiums

- Mulching to smother weeds

- Living mulch plants, such as comfrey

- Raised garden beds to control invasive weed roots

- Rotation reduces the build-up of weeds associated with various crops

- Solarisation—stretching clear plastic over a garden and sealing it for a week or more prior to sowing plants or seeds. The heat raises the soil temperature and destroys the weed seeds and plants.

CHAPTER 4

Garden Companions

Herbs, flowers, vegetables, fruits and nuts

These companion plants have proved successful for me and for dozens of fellow organic gardeners I have taught. You may find that some of the plants cannot be grown in your area due to the climate or because they are listed by your local authority as noxious weeds. However, I have provided a wide range of companions for each of the plants to cover such problems.

Where species names are incomplete or have not been included it is because there are several species.

ACEROLA or BARBADOS CHERRY (*Malpighia glabra*)
A frost-tender fruit, acerola prefers the protection of neighbouring mature fruit trees. Underplant with tansy, catmint, pineapple sage, lavender and comfrey. Allow the comfrey to die back or slash it regularly during hot months to provide the tree with a rich natural mulch. The fruit is rich in vitamin C. Acerola can be grown in tropical and subtropical areas.

AGRIMONY (*Agrimonia eupatoria*)
Once known for its 'magic' powers as a heal-all, this graceful perennial particularly enjoys the company of catmint,

foxgloves, lavender, the sage family and evening primrose. Its flowers have a delicate apricot fragrance and are made into a tea for sore throats, coughs and to treat cystitis. Agrimony yields a yellow dye. It attracts lots of bees.

AJUGA (*Ajuga reptans*)
Whenever ajuga blooms people stop and ask 'What flower is that?' The beautiful purple–blue flowers of ajuga make it a delight in any garden. It is extremely hard wearing and can withstand being walked on. Plant as a ground cover for citrus fruit. It grows well with most herbs, vegetables and flowers.

ALFALFA *(Medicago sativa)*
A companion to fruit trees and fruiting vines such as grapes and passionfruit. Grow as a ground cover under stone-fruit trees. Clippings of alfalfa are a bonus for the compost heap. Alfalfa is rich in vitamin C and its seed produces a yellow dye. Add a few leaves to a salad or cook as a vegetable.

> **Loss of appetite:** an infusion of alfalfa tea taken regularly will help.

ALMOND (*Prunus amygdalus* var. *dulcis*)
The almond tree is healthy and strong when planted in the company of escallonia, stinging nettle, catnip, garlic and sage. Escallonia, with its profuse pink blooms, invites the bees to visit the almond tree.

> **Almond soap:** mix together
> *$^1/_2$ teaspoon borax,*
> *2 tablespoons kaolin* (fine white clay),
> *2 tablespoons finely ground almonds,*

A little almond oil.
Add *rosewater* for a touch of perfume. This soap is soothing when applied like a face pack. Leave it on for a few minutes then rinse off. Great for sunburn.

ALOE VERA (*Aloe barbadensis*)

Great for skin rashes and burns—you simply squeeze the pulp directly onto the wound. In the area of natural beauty care, aloe vera is gaining a reputation as an anti-wrinkle treatment. Aloe vera enjoys the company of borage, low-growing scented geraniums, the onion family, sow thistle and balm of Gilead. Grown with elderberry, aloe vera produces plump and juicy leaves. It blends with most herbs and vegetables. Like them, it detests wet conditions.

> **Sunburn relief:** squeeze the pulp of a freshly picked leaf onto the tender skin and rub in gently. The sting will be relieved quickly.

ALPINE ANEMONE (*Anemone alpina* also known as *Pulsatilla alpina*)

While this herb is a pretty flowering plant, it is poisonous and should not be taken internally. It grows well with sow thistle, the sage family, geraniums, catmint and foxgloves.

ALYSSUM (*Alyssum*)

A colourful and happy border plant. It looks spectacular when intermingled with baby blue eyes and catnip. Use as a border plant for both the herb and the vegetable garden.

AMARANTH (*Amaranthus retroflexus*)

A soil indicator. It is regarded as a weed by many, but is respected by organic gardeners who appreciate the way its deep foraging roots aerate the soil. It is rich in vitamins A and C. Its leaves taste a little like spinach and make a delicious soup. It is a tall plant that can be most useful in an orchard.

ANGELICA (*Angelica archangelica*)

It enjoys the company of thyme, yarrow, marjoram, hollyhock and artichokes. In particular, when grown with stinging nettle its essential oil is increased by up to 80%. It enjoys the dappled light under the canopy of a stone-fruit tree or a citrus tree.

> **Travel sickness:** crushed angelica leaves help to prevent car sickness while freshening the air. Place a few in the car. Close the doors and windows and let stand for 5 minutes before setting off on your journey.

ANISE (*Pimpinella anisum*)

A highly respected culinary and medicinal herb since early Egyptian times. The germination of anise is encouraged by coriander. Cabbage worm eggs are significantly reduced when anise is planted in close proximity. Its flowers can be tossed in fruit salads and its seeds have long been used as bait in mouse traps.

> **Bronchial relief:** infuse anise seed to make a comforting antiseptic tea.

Apple (*Malus*)

Directly under the canopy of an apple tree, plant wallflowers, apple mint, chives, nasturtiums, foxgloves, marjoram and ajuga.

Apple and plum chutney

Peel, core and slice *1.4 kg apples.*
Stone and chop *1.4 kg plums.*
Chop *450 g onions.*
Place prepared fruit and onions in a heavy pan.
Add   *1.1 L brown malt vinegar,*
   450 g sultanas,
   450 g currants,
   1 teaspoon white pepper,
   1 teaspoon ground ginger,
   1 teaspoon salt,
   1 teaspoon cayenne pepper.
Mix all ingredients and heat gently, stirring until sugar has dissolved. Boil, stirring frequently, until it thickens—approximately 1 hour. When it is cooked, put aside until it is quite cold. Store in sterilised containers, making sure the lids have a good seal.

Apricot (*Prunus armeniaca*)

Plant in a bed of clover. Interplant with ginger mint, tansy, scented geraniums, horseradish, catnip, alfalfa, basil, yarrow, bush beans and Dutch medlar. Apricots dislike potatoes and tomatoes. A group planting of comfrey, chives, garlic, lucerne and horsetail grown under an apricot tree and slashed regularly will help protect it from apricot freckle.

Apricot face pack: mix fresh apricot pulp with yoghurt or buttermilk and apply to face. It cleanses and tones. It is especially good for oily skin.

ARTICHOKE, Globe (*Cynara scolymus*)

A good background plant, globe artichoke is happy among medicinal and culinary herbs that prefer moisture-retaining soil, rich in humus. In particular it grows well near hollyhock and sweet cicely. Violets are a suitable neighbouring ground cover. Since medieval times it has been recognised not only as a delicacy but also as a valuable medicinal treatment for jaundice and anaemia. It also stimulates and aids digestion. Dried flower heads can be used in floral decorations.

ARTICHOKE, Jerusalem (*Helianthus tuberosus*)

Jerusalem artichokes provide shelter for tomatoes and cucumbers. They grow well with corn, tansy and stinging nettle. When planted thickly around citrus trees they act as an insect repellent.

ASPARAGUS (*Asparagus officinalis*)

Parsley, capsicum, basil, lettuce, and tomatoes are friends of asparagus. In fact, tomatoes and asparagus stimulate each other's growth. A fast-spreading ground cover such as nasturtium acts as a sacrificial companion for insects, and provides adequate protection from weed infestation. Don't allow the nasturtiums to become too dense.

Acne blemishes: boil freshly picked young asparagus spears in milk. Apply to the problem area or to the whole of the face by patting it on with

cotton wool. Allow to dry thoroughly. You will feel it
cleansing the skin as it dries. Rinse off with tepid
water.

Nematode spray: place asparagus leaves in a blender
and puree. Add a little soapy water. Spray on
damaged asparagus and carrots or apply directly onto
the surrounding soil.

AVOCADO (*Persea americana*)
Scented geraniums, lavender, thyme, stinging nettle, southernwood and comfrey are excellent companions for
avocado. The comfrey provides a natural rich mulch and can
be slashed regularly during the hotter months.

BABY BLUE EYES (*Nemophila menziesii*)
Baby blue eyes is a friend of cats, and is often squashed by
their body weight as they love to roll and sleep amongst it. It
grows well with catmint, which also attracts cats. If you are
trying to keep cats away from precious plants, then plant
baby blue eyes at the end or corner of the garden, far from
the plants you are trying to protect. Baby blue eyes also grows
well with viola, pansies and low-growing scented geraniums.

BALM OF GILEAD (*Cedronella canariensis*)
Gipsywort, ajuga, thyme, calamint, pineapple sage, sweet
germander and soapwort make good companions for balm
of Gilead. It is a friend to aloe vera. When using it in
potpourri, add the whole bud. It has a musky aroma and is
suited to a woody type of potpourri. Balm of Gilead repels
mosquitoes.

BANANA (*Musa*)

The pawpaw tree is a good companion for banana. As a groundcover, underplant strawberries, alpine strawberries and nasturtiums.

Banana–passionfruit fruit salad:
Finely slice *2–3 medium-size bananas*.
Add the *pulp of 3 or 4 passionfruits*.
Add a *little icing sugar* (to taste) to thicken the juice from the passionfruit pulp, then toss.
Chill, and serve with whipped cream or ice cream.
This recipe is a favourite with all of my family.

BARBERRY (*Berberis darwinii, B. vulgaris*)

Tansy and catmint are suitable companions for barberry, and marjoram makes a nutritional ground cover. Barberries make an excellent preserve. Barberry jelly is eaten with mutton.

BASIL (*Ocimum basilicum*)

Recognised as an insect repellent, basil has long been associated with tomatoes. It is a companion to most vegetables and aromatic herbs. It does have one foe: rue. They will make each other very ill or kill each other. Basil helps to reduce aphids, mosquitoes, whitefly and houseflies. It also aids in the fight against invasion by the Queensland fruit fly. Plant with capsicums for a healthy crop of basil.

> **Pesto sauce:** Puree *3 cloves garlic.*
> Add alternately *1 cup fresh basil* (roughly chopped),
> *60 g pine nut kernels,*
> *60 g grated parmesan cheese.*
> Blend to a paste.
> Slowly add *¼ cup olive oil.*
> Blend until the mixture resembles a softened
> butter consistency. Season to taste with *salt*
> and *black pepper.* Serve with pasta or use as a
> topping for jacket potatoes.

> **Hair-conditioning rinse:** place basil leaves and stalks
> in a saucepan, cover with water and bring to the boil.
> Rinse through hair following shampooing to reduce
> tangles. It is a good scalp tonic too.

Bay (*Laurus nobilis*)

It has been recognised that plants neighbouring a bay tree are usually protected from both pests and disease. It is happy in the company of medicinal herbs. If you place a few bay leaves amongst stored rice, oats, rye, flour or wheat, weevils will be discouraged.

> **Stimulate hair growth:** boil fresh bay leaves in water—approximately *4 cups leaves* to *7 cups water*. Rub the tea into the scalp. Splash on the face or legs to keep roughly shaven skin soft.

Beans, Broad (*Vicia faba*)

Potatoes and broad beans have been friends for ages. They also prosper in the company of corn, viola and marjoram. Lettuce makes a suitable border plant.

Beans, Bush or Snap (*Phaseolus vulgaris*)

Fragrant herbs, feverfew and tansy are helpful insect deterrents for bean crops. Grow bush beans with corn, egg-plant, cucumbers, strawberries and celery, members of the onion family and also fennel and marigolds.

Beans, Lima (*Phaseolus limensis*)

Locust trees are helpful to lima beans. Marjoram, oregano, sow thistle and chickweed are also beneficial.

Beans, Runner (*Phaseolus coccineus*)

Watch runner beans come to life when planted among

carrots and cauliflower. Lettuce, savory, radish, corn, spinach, dwarf beans and chicory are all compatible plants. However, runner beans don't perform well when planted near sunflower, fennel, beetroot, garlic, onions, leeks and kohlrabi.

BEETROOT (*Beta vulgaris*)
This vegetable is easy to get along with. It has few enemies. You can safely interplant it with onions, kohlrabi, lettuce, spinach and silver beet.

Beetroot and alfalfa salad:
Boil *2 or 3 large beets* until tender.
Cool, peel, dice.
Combine with *1 coarsely grated carrot*,
1 sliced stick celery,
1 tablespoon parsley,
$^1/_2$ cup alfalfa sprouts,
6 finely chopped spring onions and season.
Mix approximately
300 g natural yoghurt,
1 tablespoon sugar,
2 teaspoons lemon juice to taste.
Add dressing to vegetables when serving.
Decorate with alfalfa.

BERGAMOT (*Monarda didyma*)
A well-known tea ingredient, bergamot attracts dozens of bees to the garden with its bright colourful flowers. Grow with aromatic herbs such as soapwort, lavender, feverfew, sweet germander, lemon balm and catmint.

BLACK ALDER (*Ilex verticillata*)

An elegant and versatile specimen tree for the garden and orchard, as it helps to fix nitrogen to the soil and drain wet soil.

BLUEBERRY (*Vaccinium corymbosum, V. angustifolium, V. ashei*)

I have noticed that blueberries grow exceptionally well when horehound is nearby. Blueberries require the company of companions which like acid soil. I grow one row of blueberries and one row of strawberries in a heavy mulch of pine needles.

BORAGE (*Borago officinalis*)

A tall plant, borage is best used in the background of the garden. It is highly respected for improving the flavour and size of strawberries and lettuce. Bees simply adore borage.

Decoration for cool drinks: place the dainty blue flowers of borage in an ice-cube tray with water and freeze for a decorative complement to punch and cool summer drinks.

BRACKEN (*Pteridium aquilinum*)

Stinkbugs in citrus trees are usually reduced when bracken is growing nearby. Add bracken to the compost heap or use as a nutritious plant food mulch. When burnt, the ash (potash) is valuable as fertiliser.

BROCCOLI (*Brassica oleracea*)

A very easy plant to grow, broccoli enjoys the company of onions, leeks, celery, rosemary, dill, sage, chamomile and peppermint. Harvest the broccoli heads as soon as they form, thus encouraging new heads to form.

BRUSSELS SPROUT (*Brassica oleracea* var. *bulata gemmifera*)

I always sow brussels sprouts in a carpet of thyme or pennyroyal as they are both excellent insect deterrents. For improved productivity plant sage, rosemary, lovage, hyssop and potatoes close by.

BUXUS or BOX (*Buxus sempervirens*)

Commonly used as a hedge plant for rose and herb gardens, buxus lends itself to both the formal and informal garden layout. It is also useful as a specimen plant. The box tree was very popular in Europe for its wood. Its volatile oil was once used in the treatment of toothache, while its leaves and sawdust were used to dye the hair auburn.

CABBAGE (*Brassica oleracea* var. *capitata*)

Plant cabbage seedlings in a bed of pennyroyal so that as the cabbages grow, their weight pushes down on the pennyroyal and bruises it to release its essential oil. This repels insects by disguising the aroma of the cabbage. In such a patch I would usually sow members of the onion family and thyme. Sage will help disguise the shape of the cabbages and neighbouring tomatoes will help to repel the white cabbage butterfly. A few mature bushes or a hedge of rosemary will provide a good insect repellent for the cabbage patch and most neighbouring gardens. Rue and cabbage are not compatible. Anise grown in close proximity to cabbages significantly reduces cabbage worm eggs.

CALAMINT (*Calamintha officinalis*)

Calamint grows well with sweet germander. Its leaves can be used as a poultice to relieve bruising.

CALENDULA (*Calendula officinalis*)

Calendula petals tossed in a salad add life and colour. The petals are also used as a tea, or you can boil the flowers to make a yellow dye. Old herbal remedy books commonly mention this versatile plant as pot marigold. Calendula blooms vibrantly when planted in a bed of self-heal. Plant with capsicums and tomatoes to repel insects.

Nappy rash and cradle cap: add *¹/₂ cup petals* to *1¹/₂ cups boiling water* to make a strong tea. Cool and strain. Bathe the affected area.

CAMELLIA (*Camellia japonica, C. reticulata, C. sasanqua*)

Plant a carpet of yarrow, chamomile, alyssum or baby blue eyes beneath a camellia to combat bud mite. Taller flowers and herbs should be kept at a reasonable distance so as to give camellia the air flow it requires. It likes a semi-shaded, wind-protected area. Crab apple, weigelia and magnolia are suitable neighbours.

CANDYTUFT (*Iberis*)

A pretty edging plant, candytuft adores the company of lettuce, onions, cabbage, parsley and aromatic herbs. It is most decorative when planted with catmint and chamomile.

CAPSICUM
See Peppers.

CARAWAY (*Carum carvi*)

Peas and costmary (*Chrysanthemum majus*) are complemented by caraway. This herb was used by the Egyptians as a flavouring and is known to have been in use for at least five thousand years. Caraway and fennel dislike each other.

CAROB (*Ceratonia siliqua*)

The soft delicate leaves of the ancient carob tree have endeared it to gardeners world wide. It enjoys the company of pecan, mulberry, Chinese elm, olive and chestnut. Underplant with yarrow, catnip, currants, Cape gooseberry and lemon balm.

> **Carob powder:** wash the pods and place with 1 cup water in a pressure cooker.
> Bring to pressure and simmer for 20 minutes. Cool.

Remove seeds and cut pods into pieces. Leave overnight to dry. Place the dried pieces in a blender and grind to a powder. Use as a substitute for cocoa.

CARROT (*Daucus carota* var. *sativus*)

You will get fresh, crunchy, brightly coloured carrots if you interplant them with leeks, as these two plants are the best of companions. Carrots also grow well with sage, lettuce, chives, peas, salsify, viola and rosemary.

CATMINT and CATNIP (*Nepeta mussini, N. cataria*)

Their rich lavender–blue flowers are a favourite with bees. Plant catmint (*N. mussini*) with grapes, kiwi fruit, passion-fruit, mulberry, magnolia, peach, apricot, curry plant, raspberry and carob. Catnip (*N. cataria*) attracts cats. Catnip acts as an insect repellent in the flower, vegetable and fruit garden, and an effective insect repellent spray can be made from its leaves. Research has shown that catnip reduces beetle infestation in potatoes by up to 70% and it reduces aphid infestation in sweet peppers by up to 90%.

> **Bags under the eyes:** take *60 ml catnip* and pour *½ cup boiling water* over it.
> Infuse until cooled. Strain.
> Gently apply to your eyes using a wad
> of cotton wool.

CAULIFLOWER (*Brassica oleracea* var. *botrytis*)

Remember my story of finding a cauliflower in a bed of weeds? From that lesson I learnt that cauliflower loves to grow with sow thistle, which leaches nutrients from the depths of the soil and makes them available to the cauliflower. Grow with pennyroyal or peppermint, onions, calendula, leeks, kale, yarrow, sage, thyme, valerian and lovage.

CHAMOMILE (*Anthemis nobilis, Matricaria chamomilla*)

A fragrant chamomile lawn is also an excellent insect deterrent for a neighbouring garden. Enrich the essential oils of fragrant herbs by planting chamomile nearby. Drinking chamomile tea is known by many to have a calming effect. A strong tea can be used to treat plant diseases.

> **Damping-off tea:** used to combat damping-off in seedlings. Place a handful of leaves in a bowl and cover with boiling water. Allow to cool then strain. Use as a spray.

> **Sunburn treatment:** place flowers in a bath, pour hot water over them, then cold water. Soak and relax.

CELERIAC (*Apium graveolens rapaceum*)

This vegetable is growing in popularity. Its edible root tastes like celery. Plant with lettuce, leeks, scarlet runner beans, thyme, yarrow, marjoram and oregano.

CELERY (*Apium graveolens*)

Bush beans and celery have long been friends. Tomatoes, leeks, marjoram and thyme are also compatible with celery. Blanch the celery by placing opened milk cartons over each plant.

> **Skin toner:** take several celery leaves and make them into a tea. As a wash it has a wonderful toning effect. You can also use the leaves in a bath bag.

CHERRY (*Prunus avium*)

Underplant with lavender, curry plant, catnip, tansy and marjoram. For a food-producing ground cover, plant strawberries. A nearby hedge of rosemary or wormwood will help to repel insects. Avoid pampering a cherry tree, as you can kill it with too much fertiliser and water.

CHERVIL (*Anthriscus cerefolium*)

Coriander and chervil are good mates, each complementing the other. The dainty leaves of chervil blend beautifully with sweet woodruff and viola in a garden. Chervil grows well with lettuce, chicory, marjoram and tomatoes.

CHESTNUT, Sweet (*Castanea sativa*)

The nuts of the sweet chestnut make the best stuffing for the Christmas turkey. They can be boiled, ground into flour, roasted and used in a variety of ways. Underplant this attractive tree with any of the following: catnip, tansy, feverfew, catmint, santolina. It enjoys the company of wattle, hazelnut, walnut, almond, Chinese elm, photinia and hibiscus. Neighbouring oak trees help control disease.

Boiled chestnuts: boil a pot of salted water.
Slit chestnut skins on flat side and cook until tender.
When cool enough to handle, remove shells.
Toss in melted butter and serve with poultry.

CHICORY (*Cichorium intybus*)

I love to see the bright blue flowers of chicory—they accentuate a garden by drawing your attention. Plant chicory with pennyroyal, cauliflower, lettuce, eau-de-cologne mint, parsley and chervil. Chicory aids the soil by aerating it and bringing nutrients to the surface.

CHINESE CABBAGE (*Brassica chinensis*)

These easy-to-grow cabbages enjoy the company of onions, cauliflower, lettuce and potatoes. Plant with early broad beans. Let a Chinese cabbage to go to seed to act as a trap crop for aphids.

CHIVES (*Allium schoenoprasum*)

As an insect-repellent barrier companion, I grow chives and santolina alternately in a row. I also grow it under my peach trees to combat leaf curl. Chives grow well with members of the onion and cabbage families. Chop the tops off chives regularly to deter flying insects.

> **Spray for mildew:** use this spray on squash and zucchini.
> Add *1 cup chopped chives* to *3 cups water* and bring to the boil.
> Allow to cool, then strain and dilute with equal parts of water. When applying to plants add a little soapy water (using pure soap).

CHOP SUEY (*Chrysanthemum coronarium*)

Parsley, chives, marjoram and lettuce are good companions of chop suey. I find it particularly easy to grow in filtered light under a nearby elderberry tree.

CITRUS (*Citrus*)

Delicious guava create a protective hedge for citrus trees. Underplant with lavender and catnip to protect against wood borers. Lupins and sweet pea (which fix nitrogen) help to increase the health of the tree. Ajuga and lamb's ear provide an adequate ground cover. If you encourage a grapevine to meander through a mature citrus tree it is said there will be a reduction in stinkbugs. A patch of Jerusalem artichokes planted nearby will also help to manage insects.

CLOVER (*Trifolium*)
Clover helps to repel woolly aphids. I encourage the growth of clover wherever I can, as it fixes nitrogen to the soil. I use it beneath fruit and nut trees as well as for pathways between vegetable and herb gardens. Always wear shoes and not sandals or thongs when walking in clover, as bees adore it.

COFFEE (*Coffea arabica*)
The beautiful glossy leaves of the evergreen coffee plant enrich any garden in which it is guaranteed partial shade in lush surrounds. Underplant with feverfew, sweet woodruff, violets, gota kola and ajuga. It enjoys growing near fig trees. I have found it to be very frost tender. You will enjoy its white, fragrant, star-shaped flowers.

COLLARD (*Brassica oleracea*)
A member of the cabbage family, collard enjoys the company of mints, onions, sage and thyme. Plant amongst tomatoes to control flea beetle attack on the collards. Keep it away from strawberries.

COLUMBINE (*Aquilegia vulgaris*)
Rhubarb and columbine grow well together. The abstract beauty of the spider-like flowers throws colour amongst the green of the rhubarb patch. Columbines require a well-fertilised and well-mulched garden.

COMFREY (*Symphytum officinale, S. asperum, S. grandiflorum*)

Organic gardeners have a deep respect for comfrey because of the service it offers to the garden. It's an energetic plant, growing vigorously. Comfrey likes the company of eau-de-cologne mint. It is a nutritional mulch: place a layer of comfrey leaves beneath a rose bush to help prevent rust. Grow it near fruit trees and berries so that when it dies back in the winter, it leaves a legacy of rich mulch. Comfrey is an asset in the compost bin or as a liquid fertiliser. Its medicinal applications have been documented throughout the ages.

CONIFERS

It is suggested that you avoid siting a compost heap anywhere near a hedge of conifers, which will severely inhibit its fermentation process.

COREOPSIS (*Coreopsis tinctoria*)

The happiness and vitality of coreopsis brings life to any garden. Swarms of bees hover about it in a dance of creation. Plant among parsley and low-growing scented geraniums.

CORIANDER (*Coriandrum sativum*)

Dainty coriander, with its soft foliage reminiscent of chervil or parsley, makes a decorative contribution to the cottage or herb garden. It has been cultivated for more than three thousand years. It grows well with dill and chervil. In the vegetable garden it helps to repel aphids. Anise is reputed to help coriander set seed.

CORN, Sweet or MAIZE (*Zea mays*)

I love the summer when I can walk out-doors to pick fresh

cobs of corn for lunch. Corn is usually intermingled with cucumber, melons and, of course, bush beans and peas to restore nitrogen the corn takes from the soil. On the outer edge of the corn patch there is to be found lettuce, corn salad, small peppers and bush squash. In a no-dig garden I usually grow potatoes under the mulch layer and corn on the mulch layer, interplanting with herbs and lettuce. I have found this blending of plants to produce very tasty potatoes. Growing peanuts with corn reduces borers and other pests.

CORNFLOWER (*Centaurea cyanus*)
See its pretty blooms amidst the cabbage patch, attracting bees to visit and drink its nectar, of which it is a source even in the driest weather. Cornflower is a favourite in cottage and herb gardens. It has long been identified as having a beneficial effect on small-grain crops.

CORN SALAD (*Valerianella*)
Plant parsley, chervil, corn, peppers and lettuce with corn salad. I have also found it grows well with bush melons.

COWSLIP (*Primula veris*)
Petite cowslip loves to bask in the sun with medicinal and aromatic herbs. It blends well with valerian, elderberry, English daisies and flowering bulbs.

CRESS, American (*Barbarea verna*, *B. praecox*)
This plant prefers a semi-shaded position. It enjoys the company of elderberry, cabbage and cauliflower. It is rich in vitamins and trace elements.

Cress soup: add *500 g potatoes* (peeled and diced),
1 *onion* (peeled and roughly chopped),

2 lettuce leaves (roughly chopped)
to 2^{1}/$_{2}$ *cups water.*
Simmer for approximately 1 hour.
Puree in a blender, and return to saucepan over a low heat.
Heat *2 cups milk* and stir into soup.
Puree until well blended.
Add *2 teaspoons salt*
and *1 cup finely chopped cress* (firmly packed).
Serve immediately.
For a more traditional cold cress soup simply chill, pour into chilled bowls and add a teaspoon of sour cream and a cress leaf as a garnish.

CUCUMBER (*Cucumis sativus*)

I have noticed that beans and peas stimulate the health of cucumber. I usually plant a row of radish which I allow to go to seed to ward off the cucumber beetle. In the hottest months of the year I plant cucumber amongst the corn or Jerusalem artichokes so that it receives some shelter from the harsh burning rays of the summer sun. Lettuce, kohlrabi and low-growing scented geraniums are also good companions.

Cockroach repellent: leave a few cucumber skins on the floor for about 4 days. This simple technique will deter them.

CURRANTS, Red and Black (*Ribes sativum, R. nigrum*)

Little birds love to pick the berries of currants and fly away to their nests. I plant them in among elderberry for camouflage. They enjoy the company of blueberry, strawberry and borage. Mulch well with pine needles.

Curry plant (*Helichrysum angustifolium*)
Accidentally brush against it and the aroma of curry awakens your appetite. To increase its flavour and give it added vigour, plant with foxgloves. The dried petals of the curry plant's pretty yellow flowers add colour to potpourri. A few leaves can be added to soups, stews, vegetable dishes, rice, pasta and pickles.

Dandelion (*Taraxacum officinale*)
A favourite weed because of its friendliness to earthworms. Dandelion is an excellent plant food, it activates decomposition in the compost heap and it is a nutritious mulch and a soil indicator. When I see a mature dandelion I pick a leaf to give to my pet rabbit, who thinks all her Christmases have come at once. Dandelion will always seek its own companions. However, it grows well with scented geraniums and viola. Alfalfa performs exceptionally well near dandelion. Dandelions can be used in soups, salads or as a steam vegetable. They contain nearly twice as much vitamin A, iron, calcium and phosphorus as spinach.

DATURA (*Datura officinale*)

First of all, please note that datura is poisonous to humans and animals. It benefits the garden by deterring Japanese beetle from plants that may be susceptible. A good companion is the common white geranium which also deters the Japanese beetle—together they make a formidable force.

DAY LILY (*Hemerocallis*)

Ajuga, marjoram, oregano and thyme grow well with day lily. The roots and flowers of the yellow and orange flowering varieties are used in Asian cooking. The root is sautéed, pickled and used in fritters.

DILL (*Anethum graveolens*)

Tall fern-like dill, if allowed to go to seed, will spread throughout the garden inhibiting the growth of tomatoes and carrots. Coriander and fennel enjoy its company. Dill is respected for its role in repelling the white cabbage moth and other insects. In the middle of my gardens I have an insect-repellent garden which consists of fennel, dill, feverfew, coriander, hyssop and eau-de-cologne mint.

DOCK (*Rumex obtusifolius, R. crispus*)

Recognised for relieving the sting in my favourite weed, stinging nettle. Dock is a soil indicator bringing you good news on the quality of your soil. It is an asset in the making of both liquid fertiliser and compost. Furthermore, it is a nutritious plant: leaves, seeds and roots can be eaten.

EGGPLANT (*Solanum melongera*)

To repel the potato beetles that like to nibble eggplant, plant beans nearby. Caterpillars are another pest: sprinkle eggplant with cayenne pepper each morning. Eggplant flowers don't appear to attract many bees for pollination. My solution is to interplant with columbines and sweet germander. Eggplant also grows well with peppers and lettuce.

ELDERBERRY (*Sambucus nigra*, *S. canadensis*)

In autumn elderberry shows its crowning glory in the yellow tonings of its leaves. Known through the ages as the medicine chest because all parts of the plant can be used to treat humans, animals and the garden. Most people have heard of elderberry wine, but the berries also make a health tonic rich in vitamin C. I have found that herb Robert, sweet pea, tansy, clary sage, vanilla grass and cowslip all excel near elderberry. It can also be made into a general pest-control spray. As well, it produces a light humus around its dripline: I often take a spadeful to use around ailing plants. Elderberry leaves are a valuable compost ingredient too.

> **Elderberry sauce:** place *2 apples* (peeled, cored and sliced) in a saucepan with
> *2 sprays of ripe elderberries* (taken off the stalk),
> *2 tablespoons water*,
> *1 tablespoon raw sugar*.
> Cover and simmer until the apples soften.
> Mash gently with a fork.
> This can be served hot or cold with pork
> or poultry.

ELECAMPANE (*Inula helenium*)

Very striking in the garden, this versatile plant is used in the kitchen, as a cosmetic, for medicinal purposes and is decorative. When its roots are dried they smell of sweet violets. Plant with lovage, valerian and yarrow.

Elm (*Ulmus*)

My elm trees are intermingled with fruit trees. Grapevines benefit from growing near an elm tree. The grapes usually grow larger in size and more succulent.

Evening primrose (*Oenothera biennis*)

Parsley, scented geraniums, daffodils, santolina, ajuga and marjoram are friends of the beautiful evening primrose with its healing properties.

Feijoa (*Feijoa sellowiana*)

The unique flowers of the feijoa provide a colourful border when grown in a hedge as a windbreak. Underplant with ajuga, apple mint, alpine strawberries, thyme, feverfew, catmint, alyssum or marjoram. Citrus trees enjoy the company of feijoa.

Fennel (*Foeniculum vulgare*)

Destined to be a loner. Who likes it? Eau-de-cologne mint will accommodate it. Dill and feverfew will share its space too. But most other plants can't tolerate its company as it inhibits their growth.

Fenugreek (*Trigonella foenum-graecum*)

Grow fenugreek with stinging nettle, thyme and marjoram. A yellow dye is made from its seed. Fenugreek is often used as a fodder crop.

Feverfew (*Chrysanthemum parthenium*)

The enchanting daisy-like blooms of feverfew encourage one to pick some and arrange them in a vase. A mistake! The flowers give off a fly-spray odour which takes only a few hours to completely dominate a room. Is it any wonder this vigorous plant is highly respected as an effective insect deterrent? Compatible with all its neighbours.

FLEABANE (*Erigeron*)
This plant is an excellent mosquito repellent. In my garden fleabane is planted close to the edible water gardens and the swimming pool. It grows well with yarrow, vegetables, marjoram and feverfew.

FOXGLOVE (*Digitalis purpurea*)
A cottage- and herb-garden favourite, foxglove, with its showy spray of bell-like flowers, does indeed lend an elegant flavour. Renowned for stimulating the growth of its neighbours and keeping them in the best of health. Plant foxgloves inside the canopy of an apple tree to help reduce disease.

FRENCH MARIGOLD (*Tagetes patula*)
Old time gardeners know that planting marigolds with tomatoes will increase production and improve the health of the crop. Grow with potatoes and peppers. Marigolds grow well with chrysanthemums, dahlia and calendula.

GARLIC (*Allium sativum*)
Definitely a friend of the garden as it helps to repel aphids. It is also reputed to increase the perfume in roses. I plant it under peach trees to protect them against leaf curl: the tops of the garlic must be cut regularly for it to be effective as an insect repellent. Garlic makes a good health tonic for plants, and a strong garlic tea applied to tomatoes and potatoes will control blight. You can spray it on stone-fruit trees, too, to arrest brown rot.

GERANIUM (*Pelargonium*)
Stroll along a path, brushing against an informal hedge of musk rose, rose of attar, queen of roses and peppermint rose geraniums: their scent is sweet and exquisite. Plant a mixture of lemon-, spearmint- and peppermint-scented geraniums for a more refreshing scent. Coconut, apple, nutmeg, tutti-frutti and fruit tingles are the low-growing varieties used successfully as insect repellents. The overpowering peppercorn scent of fair Ellen is an effective insect deterrent, helping to protect fruit trees. Scented geraniums and the white geranium enjoy the company of pineapple sage, ajuga, roses, camellias, mock orange, yarrow, santolina, beans, passionfruit and grapes. Plant near corn and grapes.

> **Scented bath:** for a fragrant and relaxing experience, place a few rose-scented geranium leaves in a bath. Fill with hot water to steam the oil from leaves. Then add cool water until the temperature is appropriate for bathing.

GERMANDER, Sweet or Wall (*Teucrium chamaedrys*)
Sweet germander makes an effective edging plant. It grows well with calamint, balm of Gilead, gipsywort and soapwort.

GIPSYWORT (*Lycopus europaeus*)
Gipsywort enjoys the company of balm of Gilead, sweet germander, self-heal and calamint. A black permanent dye for wool and linen is made from the fresh juice of gipsywort.

GLADIOLUS (*Gladiolus*)
Gladiolus flowers are beautiful to behold, but don't plant them densely in the vegetable patch. They inhibit the growth

of beans, peas and alfalfa: an effect is noticeable even when gladioli are planted several metres apart. Gladiolus grows well with crab apple, escallonia, ajuga, viburnum and watsonia.

GOOSEBERRY (*Ribes grossularia*)

Tansy planted near gooseberry will help to reduce insect attack, as will tomatoes. A mulch of burnt bracken will stimulate its growth.

GOOSEBERRY, Cape (*Physalis peruviana*)

Easy to identify by its paper-encased berries, this delicious fruit grows well in amongst larger fruit trees, especially plums. Tansy and catmint are good companions, as are yarrow and marjoram.

> **Cape gooseberry cocktail:** in a blender, combine
> *2 cups freshly picked cape gooseberries,*
> *1 banana,*
> *1 apple,*
> *2 cups orange juice,*
> *2 cups water,*
> *2 tablespoons desiccated coconut,*
> *honey* for sweetening.
> Serve with ice cream or natural yoghurt.

GRAPE (*Vitis, Muscadinia*)

Allow a grapevine to trail up and along the branches of an elm tree or a mulberry tree and you will have juicy, plump grapes, as these trees stimulate growth and production. A mulberry tree can be pruned regularly to make the grapes accessible for harvesting. When a grapevine intertwines with a citrus tree I have noticed that caterpillar damage is reduced substantially. Underplant grapevines with hyssop, basil, lobelia, catmint, white geranium, low-growing geraniums and ajuga. Hyssop aids in fruit yields.

Skin mask: this is for tightening and nourishing the skin. Remove pips from grapes and mash them. Apply directly to the skin and allow to firm up the skin. Rinse with lukewarm water.

Relief from fatigue: run a warm to hot bath. Add grape leaves and leave for about 4 minutes before getting into the bath. Soak in the bath for 10–15 minutes.

GUAVA, Tropical (*Psidium guajava*)

The fruit of this tree-like shrub has a high vitamin C, phosphorus and calcium content. Citrus trees are protected by and enjoy the company of guava. A blending of low-growing plants such as ajuga, marjoram and thyme provide a good ground cover.

Guava jelly: wash fruit and place in saucepan with enough water to cover the fruit. Boil moderately until the fruit is broken. Strain through jelly bag.
Add *1 cup of sugar* per cup of pulp,
plus an extra *½ cup of sugar*
and the *juice of 1 lime*.
Simmer gently until the jelly sets when tested (by dropping a small amount into a saucer of cold water). Store in sterilised jars.

GUAVA, Chilean (*Myrtus ugni*)

This small evergreen shrub makes a wonderful border plant for the vegetable patch. Underplant with catnip or santolina and chives. The Chilean guava provides shelter for low-growing vegetables and herbs. It is a substitute for cranberry in regions where the climate is not cold enough for the true cranberry. It makes a delicious wine.

HAZEL (*Corylus avellana*)

Hazel leaves are a nutritious additive to the compost heap. Suitable ground covers are yarrow, clover, and marjoram. A nearby border of tansy, catmint, southernwood, scented geraniums or wormwood is a beneficial insect deterrent. Hazel grows well in the company of other nut trees. Grown in a hedge it is less susceptible to hazelnut blight. It thrives on mulch made from its own leaves. Hazelnut is reputed to be a good fodder for cattle.

Herb Robert (*Geranium robertianum*)

Herb Robert enjoys the filtered light and the rich humus provided by an elderberry tree. It has a reputation in folklore as a favourite plant of fairies and goblins.

Hollyhock (*Althaea rosea*)

Hollyhock enjoys the company of angelica, artichokes and pineapple sage. It is best to plant it next to a sunny wall or a secure stake because of its size and the weight of its flowers. It is a wonderful background plant for the herb garden.

Horehound (*Marrubium vulgare*)

The soft grey foliage of horehound makes a delicate trimmed hedge. It has a reputation for repelling grasshoppers and aphids. It is compatible with peach and mulberry trees, santolina and low-growing scented geraniums such as the coconut geranium. Horehound was commonly used to make a tonic for a sore throat, and a tea made from horehound leaves is reputed to help you lose weight.

Horseradish (*Armoracia rustica*)

Please a mulberry tree or peach tree by planting horseradish nearby. Increase a potato crop by interplanting with horseradish. It also enjoys the company of sorrel, sweet germander, feverfew and sweet violet.

Horsetail (*Equisetum arvense*)

Horsetail is compatible with members of the sage family. It grows well with germander, scented geraniums, mugwort, marjoram and yarrow. Its silica content makes an excellent spray for fungal diseases. Plant at the back of the herb or vegetable garden.

HYACINTH (*Hyacinthus orientalis*)
This colourful plant grows well with crab apple, tulip, fruit trees, magnolias and mulberry. Both the white and blue hyacinth are mildly fragrant. It has a way of highlighting other plants in the garden.

HYSSOP (*Hyssopus officinale*)
Grapes and hyssop have long been planted together—the yield of the grapevine is greatly increased by the presence of hyssop. It is a lure for the cabbage butterfly, and bees love it too. Make a tea from hyssop to combat diseases caused by bacteria.

JASMINE (*Jasminum officinale*)
Grow jasmine with rhubarb, elderberry, perennial wall-flower, crepe myrtle and fig. Its fragrance abounds with vitality for life.

> **Aching feet:** infuse jasmine flowers in white
> vinegar to make a fragrant and soothing bath
> for your feet.

KALE (*Brassica oleracea acephala*)
Plant kale with potatoes and corn; otherwise, treat it as you would cabbages. It dislikes strawberries and beans.

KIWI FRUIT (*Actinidia deliciosa*)
Marjoram and catnip (low-growing variety) will provide a supportive ground cover. Larger herbs such as lemon balm, scented geraniums, currants, lavender, lemon verbena and white geranium are ideal companions.

KOHLRABI (*Brassica oleracea caulorapa*)

Beans and kohlrabi dislike each other. Kohlrabi is enhanced by beetroot and members of the onion family as well as marjoram, oregano, the mint family, tansy, sage and thyme.

LARKSPUR (*Delphinium consolida*)

A stately plant, larkspur is at home in the vegetable, herb or cottage garden. It is recognised as an insect repellent, particularly for the control of aphids and thrips. Plant with scented geraniums and nasturtiums.

LAVENDER (*Lavandula officinalis*)

Perennial wallflower stimulates the flower production of lavender. Place these two plants in partnership and both will grow beyond average size. Clover is a suitable groundcover companion. Rosemary, tansy, catmint and feverfew are also compatible. Grow a pot of lavender near a doorway to deter flies, or a hedge of lavender near an outdoor toilet or laundry.

> **Lavender tea:** pour *1 cup boiling water* over
> *1 teaspoon leaves or flowers.*
> Stand for approximately 5 minutes.
> Strain and sweeten with honey.

LEEKS (*Allium porrum*)

Members of the cabbage family grow well with leeks, as do carrots, celery and celeriac. I find alternate rows of celery, onions and leeks are most successful.

LEMON BALM (*Melissa officinalis*)

Grow with passionfruit and watch both plants flourish. When lemon balm is grown near tomatoes, their growth and flavour are improved. Balm also grows well with members of the onion family, feverfew, calendula, thyme, lemon grass, scented geraniums and tansy, and with carob and citrus trees. Add this delicious herb to chilled summer drinks, fruit salads and salad dressings. Lemon balm tea with a little honey is reputed to give you increased vigour.

> **Lemon balm cheesecake:** use this delicious filling with your favourite pastry recipe.
> Cream together *50 g margarine*,
> *30 ml honey*,
> *350 g cream cheese*.
> Beat in *2 eggs*.
> Fold some *finely chopped lemon balm* (to taste) into the mixture.
> Pour into a pastry case or cheesecake base and bake for approximately 45 minutes, or until the filling has set.

LEMON VERBENA (*Aloysia triphylla*)

Brush up against a lemon verbena bush and breathe in its rich fragrance, reputed to repel flying insects. Plant amongst kiwi fruit, passionfruit and gooseberry.

Lemon verbena tea: place *6 dried lemon verbena leaves* into a teapot and pour *250 ml boiling water* over them.
Infuse for a few minutes and drink hot.
It may be sweetened with honey.

LETTUCE (*Lactuca sativa*)

Try planting lettuce in a dappled light in the hottest months of the year. You will be rewarded with a succulent crop. Interplant with strawberries, beetroot or radish to enhance their flavour. Lettuce is compatible with most plants. Each year I plant lettuce in amongst the corn crop. As the corn grows it shades the lettuce; as the lettuce get larger they act as an anchor for the corn during heavy winds. This system works very well.

LILLY PILLY (*Acmena smithii*)

Amongst my childhood memories is a lilly pilly tree which grew in my grandmother's backyard; my cousin David and I used to sit in the tree nibbling the tart berries. These are also really delicious when preserved. Yarrow, horehound and catmint are good companions.

LOBELIA (*Lobelia inflata*)

Underneath my grapevines I have a mixture of lobelia, alyssum, catmint and baby blue eyes. Lobelia, with its rich purple–blue flowers, always gives a cheerful lift to the garden.

LOQUAT (*Eriobotrya japonica*)

A dense good-looking tree producing delicious fruit. It is also known as the Japanese medlar. It benefits from growing near perennial wallflower, escallonia, mulberry and Dutch medlar. This fruit is delicious eaten raw and freshly picked. It is suitable for fruit salads and jellies.

LOVAGE (*Levisticum officinale*)
The nurturing qualities of lovage are unsurpassed. It is a friend to all its neighbours, especially vegetables.

> **Lovage soup:** Melt 25 *g butter* and
> sauté 2 *finely chopped medium onions*.
> Add 4 *tablespoons finely chopped lovage leaves*.
> Stir in 25 *g plain flour*.
> Slowly add 550 *ml chicken stock*.
> Simmer for 15 minutes.
> Add 600 *ml milk* and season to taste.
> Slowly reheat but don't allow to boil.

LUPIN (*Lupinus luteus*, *L. polyphyllus*)
Sown in garden beds or in the orchard, lupins regenerate the soil through an abundance of nitrogen nodules which fix nitrogen in the soil and stimulate the growth of neighbouring plants. They also attract earthworms.

LYCHEE (*Litchi chinensis*)
Underplant with comfrey, to be slashed regularly and left to die back as a nutritional mulch. Lavender, rosemary, scented geraniums and lemon grass are also beneficial.

MACADAMIA (*Macadamia tetraphylla*, *M. integrifolia*)
My macadamia tree is underplanted with comfrey for a nutritional mulch, a hedge of fair Ellen geranium and catmint as insect deterrents, plus ajuga as a ground cover.

MANGO (*Mangifera indica*)

Where would summer be without the succulent, juice-dripping mango? It is an age-old plant, respected and used in ceremonies by the Hindu religion. It grows well with alpine strawberry, garlic, lavender and rosemary.

MARJORAM (*Origanum majorana*)

A nurturing companion, marjoram helps all plants to grow strong and healthy and to improve their flavour. It is an asset in the vegetable garden.

MELON

Potatoes and melons are rivals, inhibiting each other's growth. Corn and sunflowers are ideal companions for melon —I let a melon vine wind its way through the corn patch.

MIGNONETTE (*Reseda odorata*)

A highlight of herb gardens, sweet mignonette complements aromatic herbs, alpine strawberries, sweet violets and ajuga.

MINT (*Mentha*)

Common mint and basil mint enhance the flavour and health of tomatoes and cabbages. They also repel aphids.

Candied mint leaves: wash and drain mint leaves.
Remove them carefully from the stem.
Beat an egg white and apply to both sides of the leaves using a pastry brush.
Dip in castor sugar.
Lay the leaves on greaseproof paper and dry slowly in an oven, turning them from time to time.

MOCK ORANGE (*Philadelphus coronarius* 'Virginal', 'Sybille', 'Etoile Rose')

Plant mock orange amongst fruit trees to encourage bees and to provide an uplifting fragrance. It grows well with dogwood, viburnum, abelia and photinia.

MULBERRY (*Morus alba*, *M. rubra*)

Grapes and chokoes increase their yield when planted near mulberry and can be trained to grow up the tree. Curry plant, tarragon, loquat, sweet violet and horseradish are also compatible.

Sopa de amoras: this soup comes from Brazil.
Rinse *900 g ripe mulberries* and place in saucepan.
Add *¹/₂ bottle of white wine* and enough water to cover.
Bring to boil over moderate heat and simmer gently until mushy. Stir occasionally.
Remove pan from heat and add *1 teaspoon cinnamon* and *sugar* to taste.

Heat through but do not boil.

Serve immediately with dry toast.

MUSTARD (*Brassica alba*)

Mustard and alfalfa are commonly sown together in orchards to assist the growth of the trees. I sow it amongst grapevines as well. Toss the mustard flowers in salads.

NASHI PEAR (*Pyrus pyrifolia, P. ussuriensis*)

Delicious, mouth-watering nashi fruit, apple pear or Asian pear delights in growing with foxgloves, perennial wall-flower, stinging nettle, sow thistle, escallonia, mulberry, apple, loquats and its fellow pear trees. Fruit ripens on the tree. This tree is easy and quick to grow and can be grown in a container. They also adapt well as espaliers along an ornamental frame, a fence or wall. The large white flowers are eye catching, and in autumn the leaves turn deep purple. The fruit is usually expensive to purchase in the shops, yet so easy to grow at home. This is a worthwhile specimen and fruiting tree for a garden or balcony.

NASTURTIUM (*Tropaeolum majus*)

Plant nasturtiums well away from plants that are afflicted by aphids, because nasturtiums attract them. Remember, they are a sacrificial companion plant (although the red and orange varieties are less susceptible), luring aphids away from susceptible plants. Planted with sweet peppers they help to reduce aphid attack by almost half. Sow orange nasturtiums amongst squash. Some organic gardeners plant nasturtiums amongst potatoes too, with good results. It grows rapidly yet places little nutritional demand on neighbouring plants or the soil. I use it as a living mulch for asparagus.

NECTARINE (*Prunus persica* var. *nucipersica*)

Each year I am seen to hover around the nectarine tree ensuring it is safe and well. I love to eat freshly picked nectarines, that is why I am so dedicated to this specimen. When you are looking to provide it with suitable companions treat it the same way you would a peach tree.

OKRA (*Hibiscus esculentus*)

Grow with members of the sage family and other aromatic herbs. It adds a particularly decorative look at the rear of a cottage or herb garden.

OLIVE (*Olea europaea*)

This old-fashioned plant grows well with pistachio, wattle, chestnut, almond and walnut. The grey–green leaves of the olive tree are highlighted when planted near mature citrus trees. Underplant with tansy, rosemary, lavender and horehound for pest management.

ONION (*Allium cepa*)

Each time I have to plant out onions I immediately think of cabbage and carrots, as these two plants make great companions. A successful border companion is lettuce. I also ensure that chamomile and summer savory are nearby. Keep onions away from peas and beans or their growth will be inhibited—one or two onions don't hurt, but a whole onion patch will.

ORACH (*Atriplex hortensis*)

Known as French spinach to many, this old herb is reputed to reduce swelling of the glands when placed on the throat. Grows well with most aromatic and medicinal herbs, as well as vegetables.

Oregano (*Origanum vulgare*)

I have found that oregano does much to repel the white butterfly that afflicts members of the cabbage family. Oregano stimulates the health and flavour of broccoli. It is a nurturing companion and is therefore compatible with numerous plants.

Pansy, Wild (*Viola tricolor*)

Dainty viola abounds with life and vigour when planted near carrots. Decoratively, it blends well with baby blue eyes, alyssum and catmint. Plant with cabbages, onions, lettuce, broad beans and elderberry.

Parsley (*Petroselinum hortense*)

Parsley is a friend to many plants. In particular, both asparagus and tomatoes excel in the presence of parsley. Parsley becomes an insect repellent when planted with carrots. Improve the health and vigour of parsley by interplanting with peppermint.

> **Parsley butter:** soften butter and add finely chopped parsley to taste. It is delicious on potatoes in their jackets and on fish.

Parsnip (*Pastinaca sativa*)

There are few plants that don't enjoy the company of the parsnip. A reliable planting system is to alternate rows of lettuce, chive or shallots and parsnip—it works well for my garden.

Passionfruit (*Passiflora*)

Underplant a passionfruit vine with marjoram so that it can be nurtured throughout its life. Lemon balm and scented geraniums, lemon grass and eau-de-cologne mint are also good companions.

Passionfruit punch: boil *600 ml water* and *2 cups sugar* to make a syrup.
Pour it over the *pulp of 12 passionfruit.*
Add *1 teaspoon citric acid.*
Stir and blend all ingredients.
Stand until cold, strain and chill in refrigerator.
Serve with iced water to taste.

PAWPAW and PAPAYA (*Asimina triloba, Carica papaya*)

Pawpaw requires a sunny sheltered area protected from frost. Strawberries, bananas, ajuga and marjoram seem to make especially good companions.

PEA (*Pisum sativum*)

Members of the onion family inhibit the growth of peas so be aware. They grow well with radish, cucumber, carrots, sweet corn, beans and turnips. I grow peas and potatoes together and find them a helpful combination.

PEACH (*Prunus persica*)

Where I live peach trees grow wild on the side of the road, often producing small yet delicious fruit. On close inspection, I always find an assortment of nutritious weeds nearby. I plant lavender, garlic, tansy, horseradish, horehound, chamomile, marjoram, sweet violet, hellebore and tarragon within the canopy of a peach tree to deter a number of threatening insects. Allow the tree to breathe: don't place the taller plants too close to the trunk of the tree. Strawberries are an ideal groundcover as they repel the oriental fruit moth.

Emollient: run a hot bath and add some peach leaves. Allow to stand for 5 minutes before you take your 15-minute bath.

PEANUT (*Arachis hypogaea*)

Most commonly used as a ground cover crop in a young orchard, as it is leguminous. Peanuts require a heavy mulch to prevent loss of moisture.

PEAR (*Pyrus*)

Don't let grass grow inside the dripline of the tree as it may inhibit its growth. Our pear trees thrive with stinging nettle nearby and other friends such as scented geranium, tansy, catmint and sage. Don't grow hawthorn near a pear tree as it attracts the pear and cherry slug.

PECAN (*Carya illinoinensis*)

I like to grow pecan amongst stinging nettle and see it flourish. As the nettle is about to go to seed, I slash it and rake it around the tree to act as a nutritious mulch. Clover is a beneficial companion too. Underplant with tansy and catmint.

PENNYROYAL (*Mentha pulegium*)

I keep a bed of pennyroyal so that I can grow members of the cabbage family successfully in it. As cauliflower and cabbage grow in size, their weight bruises the pennyroyal and releases its essential oils into the atmosphere to repel insects.

PEPINO (*Solanum muricatum*)

Plant pepino beneath a mulberry tree and watch it thrive in the partial shade. It also requires protection from the wind and frost. Marjoram, oregano and thyme are beneficial groundcover companions.

PEPPERMINT (*Mentha piperita*)
My friend the stinging nettle increases the oil content in peppermint. Parsley grows rich and healthy near peppermint. Members of the cabbage and onion family are also good companions.

> **Peppermint tea:** pour *250 ml boiling water* onto
> *2 teaspoons peppermint leaves.*
> Cover and infuse for several minutes.
> If preferred, sweeten with honey.

PEPPER, Chilli (*Capsicum frutescens*, var. *fasiculatum* and var. *longum*)
I find this plant self-sows easily in my garden. It is compatible with most vegetables. Intermingle with sweet peppers (capsicum) lettuce, squash, cucumber and viola.

PEPPER, Sweet (*Capsicum frutescens* var. *grossum*)

I choose to grow sweet peppers with basil, tomatoes, rhubarb, eggplant, lettuce, asparagus, parsley, silver beet, scented geraniums, okra and spinach. I find the combination of capsicum and eggplant very beneficial. US research has shown that when sweet peppers are planted with catnip there is a 90% reduction in aphids, and a 40% reduction if they are planted with nasturtiums.

> **Spray for cucumber:** boil a few small sweet peppers in a litre of water.
> Cool and strain.
> Add a little soapy water (using only pure soap).
> Use to treat cucumber mosaic.

PERSIMMON (*Diospyros*)

The persimmon tree has decorative bark, and provides an ornamental feature in the garden. It does well in the presence of marjoram, garlic, chives, comfrey, catmint, sage, mints and tansy.

PINE (*Pinus*)

Pine needles promote soil acidity; consequently they offer a nutritious mulch, as well as partial shelter, for both blueberry and strawberry.

PISTACHIO (*Pistacia vera*)

This small bush-like tree is relatively easy to grow and provides a lively autumn spray of colour. It grows well with chestnut, wattle, almond and hazelnut. Plant rosemary and horehound nearby.

PLUM (*Prunus domesticas, P. salicina*)
A popular fruit tree which should be interplanted with stinging nettle, catnip, tansy, scented geraniums, garlic and chives. Southernwood or wormwood should be planted outside the drip line of the tree as an insect repellent.

POTATO (*Solanum tuberosum*)
To help protect potatoes from potato blight, plant tomatoes nearby—but remember that the potatoes may slow the growth of the tomato plant. The risk of blight is further reduced by planting sunflower and cucumber. Potatoes enjoy the company of orach too. Green beans and peas are beneficial partners for potatoes, as are broad beans.

Bruising: place raw potato on bruises to remove discolouration.

PUMPKIN (*Cucurbita*)
I let a pumpkin vine meander through the corn patch and around my citrus fruit trees. When the vine dies back it provides a healthy mulch. I keep it away from potatoes as it is not usually compatible.

PYRETHRUM (*Chrysanthemum cinerariifolium*)
This grey fern-like plant with its elegant foliage and sprays of white daisies should be planted amongst strawberries to act as a pest deterrent.

QUANDONG (*Santalum acuminatum*)
This native tree is related to sandalwood, and grows to roughly the same shape and size as a peach tree. Both the

flesh and the nut are eaten. Plant near stinging nettle, rosemary and lavender.

QUINCE (*Cydonia oblonga*)
I originally planted this tree for my mother who has childhood memories of eating quince. It is delicious stewed. I underplant with numerous garlic plants to enhance the flavour of the fruit.

RADISH (*Raphanus sativus*)
If you like your radish hot then plant chervil nearby; if you like a more moderate flavour plant nasturtium. Lettuce tends to make radish more tender. The partnership between radish and peas is of mutual benefit, as is radish and kohlrabi. On the other hand hyssop and radish dislike each other immensely. Apart from that, radish helps most plants.

RANUNCULUS (*Ranunculus*)
Plant ranunculus with daffodils, English daisies, pansies, hyacinths, viola, ajuga and tulips for a wonderful effect.

RAPE (*Brassica napus, B. campestris oleifera*)
Rape, now known as canola, improves soil drainage, making soil more friable and helping to correct soil damage.

RASPBERRY (*Rubus idaeus*)
Plant alternate rows of raspberry and tansy with a scattering of rue as a pest deterrent. Harlequin beetles, which suck the juice out of raspberries until the fruit is hard and useless, can be lured away with a sacrificial crop of turnips. I find that training raspberry along a lattice fence enables easy pruning

and harvesting. Raspberry dislikes blackberry and causes blight in potatoes.

> **Raspberry sauce:** rub *450 g fresh raspberries* through a sieve and discard seeds.
> Beat in some *lemon juice*.
> Add *2–3 tablespoons icing sugar*, to taste.
> Chill.
> Pour over fruit salad or ice cream.

RHUBARB (*Rheum rhaponticum*)

I grow rhubarb with jasmine, sweet cicely, columbines, peppers and geraniums. Keep the area free of dock as it attracts insects which affect rhubarb plants.

ROSE (*Rosa*)

Garlic is a well-known companion of roses. I don't use it. Instead I plant a low border hedge of santolina and chives, which I trim regularly to expel their scent. This deters pests and stimulates the perfume of the rose. I mulch with comfrey leaves to combat disease. Rose vinegar makes a good natural deodorant.

ROSEMARY (*Rosmarinus officinalis*)

In ancient Greek temples, rosemary was burnt as an offering to the gods and goddesses. It was also used in bridal wreaths to promote love. But the exciting thing for the gardener about this favourite old-fashioned herb is that its leaves repel sap-sucking insects while its flowers attract predators. Sage and rosemary stimulate each other's growth and health. Beans, cabbage and carrots benefit from rosemary too. Potatoes do not. Plant a hedge of rosemary around the garden and plant prostrate rosemary along pathways among fruit trees. Inhaling the scent of rosemary stimulates concentration. I burn rosemary oil while writing books and always when I am teaching courses.

RUE (*Ruta graveolens*)

Grow in among raspberry plants to protect them against pests or near the compost bin to repel flies. Basil and rue are rivals and should not be planted together as neither will flourish. Sage and rue dislike each other as well, and rue should not be grown near cabbages.

SAGE (*Salvia officinalis*)

Sage's best friend in the garden is rosemary: they stimulate each other's growth and health. Members of the cabbage family and carrots benefit from growing close to sage. Rue and sage are incompatible.

SAGE, Pineapple (*Salvia elegans*)
A fragrant plant with striking blooms. The leaves can be added to drinks and fruit dishes, and it also repels sap-sucking insects. All this in one beautiful plant! It grows well with dyer's chamomile, santolina, ajuga, scented geraniums and azalea. Small birds are attracted by pineapple sage.

SAGE, Mexican or Spanish (*Salvia lavandulifolia*)
When Mexican sage is in bloom people stop and stare at its deep blue velvety flowers, soft and smooth to the touch. It repels sap-sucking insects. Plant among elderberry, scented geranium, tansy, sweet germander, curry bush and foxglove. A bed of Mexican sage is an asset situated next to a vegetable patch that is susceptible to aphids.

SALAD BURNET (*Poterium sanguisorba*)
I am often to be found in garden chewing on a leaf of salad burnet, and when I conduct tours of my garden I share it around. It has a similar flavour to cucumber. Salad burnet stimulates the growth of mint and thyme.

SALSIFY (*Tragopogon porrifolius*)
Plant alternate rows of carrots, onions and salsify for a beneficial effect. Salsify is reputed by organic gardeners to repel the carrot fly.

SANTOLINA (*Santolina chamaecyparissus*)
This plant offers you a choice. You can select the soft pale grey variety or the rich dense green, depending on the

decorative effect you want. Either one provides a low, insect-repellent hedge which can be trimmed or left to grow naturally. It enjoys the company of chives, sorrel, low-growing scented geraniums and ajuga. Santolina stimulates the perfume in roses.

SAPODILLA (*Manilkara zapota*)
Plant sapodilla with mature trees and tall medicinal herbs to protect it from the frost. It enjoys the company of mulberry and hibiscus. If you have never tasted sapodilla, let me tempt you. It has a sweet, caramel-flavoured fruit. Don't plant it too close to banana trees, or the sapodilla may encounter the problems of the banana.

SAVORY, Summer and Winter (*Satureia hortensis*, *S. montana*)
Summer savory stimulates the growth of onions. Use winter savory in a border near beans to repel the bean beetle.

SCOTCH BROOM (*Cytisus scoparius*)
Organic gardeners recognise the value of Scotch broom in accumulating calcium. It is a valuable ingredient for the compost heap.

SELF-HEAL or WOUNDWORT (*Prunella vulgaris*)
When self-heal blooms it provides a pink blanket of colour. I have found it grows very well close to calendula and motherwort. It is commonly used as a mouthwash and a gargle for mouth ulcers and sore throats.

SHALLOT (*Allium ascalonicum*)
The cabbage family, as well as beetroot, carrots, mint, sage

and thyme, are suitable companions. The growth of peas and beans will be inhibited if planted near shallots.

SILVER BEET (*Beta vulgaris* var. *cicla*)

A very accommodating plant, silver beet is compatible with most plants. It grows well with members of the onion family, beetroot, borage and parsnip. I also grow it amongst Italian lavender and find it excels.

SNAPDRAGON (*Antirrhinum*)

This attractive cottage garden plant does well when planted amongst baby blue eyes, parsley, spinach, viola, sage, alyssum, catmint and throughout the vegetable garden. Place fresh snapdragon flowers in a bath bag to soothe chafed skin.

SOAPWORT (*Saponaria officinalis*)

I have lost count of how many people I encourage, when they are touring my garden, to get on their hands and knees and enjoy the subtle perfume of soapwort. Its blooms add a soft touch to the garden. It grows well with angelica, self-heal, sweet germander and catmint.

SORREL (*Rumex acetosa*)

Sorrel thrives in the company of lettuce and onions. It also likes horseradish, santolina, spinach, silver beet and chives.

SOUTHERNWOOD (*Artemisia abrotanum*)

This powerful insect repellent is best planted outside the dripline of a fruit tree: its roots can be toxic and will inhibit the development of young fruit trees. Don't plant it directly in the garden—it inhibits vegetables and herbs alike—but as a hedge in a windy area so that it is bruised by the elements. In this way it can easily release its aroma to repel pests. It does not inhibit marguerite daisy, catmint, elderberry or members of its own family such as wormwood, tarragon and the beautiful fern-like Roman wormwood.

> **Stimulate hair growth:** add *1 cup chopped southernwood* to *1 cup boiling water*.
> Stand for 1–3 minutes.
> Strain and rub into scalp.

SPEARMINT (*Mentha spicata*)
Spearmint in the garden often means a reduction in aphids as it is efficient in its role as an insect repellent. It can be invasive if not kept in check.

SPINACH (*Spinacia oleracea*)
I find spinach to be a fairly compatible plant and manage to interplant it with numerous plants. It enjoys the company of strawberries, santolina and sorrel.

STINGING NETTLE (*Urtica dioica, U. urens, U. incisa*)
Everyone who attends any of my lectures soon learns that stinging nettle is my favourite companion plant. It is commonly recognised by organic gardeners as being one of the most valuable plants in an ecologically balanced garden. The essential oils in aromatic herbs are increased when stinging nettle is nearby. Furthermore, it improves the health of fruit trees and vegetables generally. Clumps of this wonderful herb are to be found about my gardens. Its versatility seems never ending: it produces a super liquid fertiliser; it makes a

superb compost; when cut, it provides a rich, nutritious mulch; it is a medicinal treatment for animals and humans. I use the sludge at the bottom of the liquid fertiliser bin as a healing paint for damaged limbs in fruit trees.

STRAWBERRY (*Fragaria*)

To me, a walk in the garden to pick and eat the sweet and juicy strawberry is what an edible landscape is all about. My strawberry patch is littered with borage plants to enhance the flavour and juice of the strawberries. I also grow lettuce, bush beans, silver beet and spinach amongst my strawberries. Marigolds or pyrethrum growing nearby will act as an insect repellent, and a mulch of pine needles will aid the patch too. Small birds can often mutilate the strawberries, so watch out. Strawberries grown as a groundcover beneath a peach tree can protect it from the oriental fruit moth by attracting fruit-moth parasites.

SUNFLOWER (*Helianthus annuus*)

Next time you see a sunflower look at the way it smiles at you. It is a bright chirpy plant. It makes a good windbreak, protecting vulnerable plants. Sweet corn and sunflowers are compatible, as they reduce each other's susceptibility to pest invasion. Cucumber is a friend that should be allowed to ramble throughout the sunflowers, but potatoes and sunflowers inhibit each other's development and should be kept apart.

> **Dry skin pack:** grind *500 ml sunflower seed* with *milk* until it forms a paste.
> Apply and leave on the face for approximately 20 minutes.
> Remove with warm water.

SWEDE or RUTABAGA (*Brassica naprobrassica*)

Swedes don't like growing with potatoes or mustard. They prefer the company of peas, viola, lettuce and members of the onion family.

SWEET CICELY (*Myrrhis odorata*)

Rhubarb loves the companionship of sweet cicely, as do angelica, lovage and artichokes. Its roots were once boiled or steamed and allowed to cool, then eaten in salads. The leaves may be added to soups.

TAMARILLO (*Cyphomandra betacea*)

Peppers, basil, thyme, marjoram, ajuga and low-growing

scented geraniums are all compatible with tamarillo. I have found that it responds well to a regular mulch of comfrey leaves which helps it retain its much-needed moisture. As well as providing a rich source of plant food, tamarillo is a good source of vitamin C.

TANSY (*Tanacetum vulgare*)

Where would the companion-planted garden be without good old reliable tansy, defending its neighbours against pests and disease? It's a vital companion for fruit trees as it deters most harmful flying insects. Tansy and lavender make a good insect-repellent team for citrus trees. It also helps bramble berries, the cabbage family and roses. I underplant my orange trees with tansy to sweeten the juice of the fruit. Tansy is most compatible.

TARRAGON (*Artemisia dracunculus*, *A. dracunculoides*)

To increase the vitality of either Russian or French tarragon, plant beneath a mulberry tree. It has mild insect-repellent abilities, but its contribution to the kitchen should ensure it a place in all edible gardens. Sweet violets grow well with tarragon.

THYME (*Thymus vulgaris*)

Thyme is another friendly companion, helping all of its neighbours to good health. It enjoys the company of the cabbage family, the onion family and sage. It helps to repel cabbage worm. Thyme is stimulated by salad burnet.

> **Skin rash:** add *3 cups boiling water* to *1 cup thyme*.
> Let stand for 5 minutes.
> When cooled sufficiently, apply to the affected area.

TOMATO (*Lycoperiscon esculentum*)
I find that peppers and tomatoes make a harmonious team; similarly, asparagus and tomatoes. Basil is a helpful insect-repellent friend. Tomatoes dislike kohlrabi, fennel and potatoes. Columbine will attract red spiders, who will make a meal of the tomatoes.

TURNIP (*Brassica campestris* var. *rapa*)
Don't plant turnips close to either mustard or potatoes, as they won't thrive. Their mutual friends are peas, beans, viola and chives. Plant turnips as a decoy to attract harlequin beetles away from raspberries.

VALERIAN (*Valeriana officinalis*)
Valerian is compatible with a huge number of plants. It stimulates phosphorus where it grows, and vegetables grown near valerian excel. Its root stock is used in soups.

VETCH (*Vicia*)
A legume, vetch improves the soil by increasing its nitrogen content. It is mainly employed in orchards where it is allowed to grow, then slashed and left as a mulch.

VIOLET, Sweet (*Viola odorata*)
Outside my back door I keep a circular garden of sweet violets, so that their perfume can waft through the house. Sweet violet is a companion to many plants, including sweet woodruff, ajuga, crab apple, elderberry, mulberry, tarragon and low-growing geraniums.

> **Tea for colds:** add *315 ml boiling water* to *1 teaspoon dried violet flowers.*

Cover and infuse for approximately 5 minutes. Strain and sweeten with honey.

WALLFLOWER (*Cheiranthus cheiri*)

I underplant my apple tree with perennial wallflowers and find they do a wonderful job of reducing woolly aphids. When planted next to lavender, perennial wallflower not only doubles in size, it blooms profusely too.

WALNUT, Black (*Juglans nigra*)

Don't grow this tree with apples, alfalfa, asparagus, berries, chrysanthemum, dock, potatoes, tomatoes, azaleas, rhododendrons or pine trees, as none of these plants thrive in its company. It grows well with wattle, stinging nettle and horsetail.

WALNUT, English (*Juglans regia*)

Underplant English walnut with angelica, spearmint, apple mint, sweet woodruff, violets and anise. It is not as toxic as its brother the black walnut. Outside the canopy of the tree, plant a wide variety of flowering bulbs. Companion plants have no effect on cankers but stinging nettle helps to reduce bacterial blight.

WATERMELON (*Citrullus vulgaris*)

I plant watermelon amongst my citrus trees and corn and pumpkin vines. I find these three combinations work very well indeed. Melon leaves are rich in calcium and should end up in the compost bin, where they make a valuable contribution.

WATTLE (*Acacia*)

The bright blooms of wattle light up our orchard. At the same time we know they are busy bringing nitrogen from the air and fixing it in the soil. Wattle is short lived and therefore can provide protection for young fruit trees that may be susceptible to the environment while they are learning to acclimatise. However, don't plant young trees and shrubs too close to wattle roots and branches: they will compete for moisture, light and nutrients.

WOODRUFF, Sweet (*Asperula odorata*)

The subtle fragrance of sweet woodruff lingers outside my bedroom window. Its leaves are decorative and it looks soft and delicate at the foot of the tree ferns. My apple trees, lemon grass, violets and white hellebore are all companion planted with sweet woodruff.

WORMWOOD (*Artemisia absinthium*)

Because of its toxic roots, wormwood is usually sentenced to some distant place in the garden. Although it is an excellent insect repellent, it does inhibit the growth of most neighbouring plants. I grow it as a hedge near the citrus trees. It is also planted throughout the orchard, but always outside the dripline of trees, so as not to affect them. Wormwood should be grown in a raised garden bed or in a windy corridor so that its leaves can be bruised by the elements in order to release its pest-deterring aroma. I grow wormwood in an old 44-gallon drum in my vegetable garden. You will find that jasmine, elderberry and marguerite daisy will tolerate its company.

YARROW (*Achillea millefolium*)

The benefits of yarrow are recognised by organic gardeners, who see it as a exceptional plant. It stimulates the health and growth of aromatic and medicinal herbs particularly, but assists in maintaining the health of all its neighbours. I grow cauliflowers in a bed of yarrow and peppermint: year after year they are plump and healthy. Yarrow can also be used in pathways between vegetable gardens.

ZUCCHINI or COURGETTE (*Curcurbita pepo* var. *melopepo*)

I find that zucchini will tolerate a large number of herb and vegetable neighbours. In particular: lettuce, peppermint, peppers (capsicum), corn, silver beet, spinach, squash, tomatoes and parsley.

CHAPTER 5

Using the Companion-planted Garden

As a companion-planted garden matures it requires a little trimming from time to time, providing an abundance of foliage that offers a nutritious food source for the garden. Nothing is ever wasted in the companion-planted garden because everything in the system has a purpose. Prunings are used as mulch, compost ingredients, liquid fertiliser, insect repellent and disease-control treatments.

COMPOSTING WITH COMPANION PLANTS

MAKING COMPOST

1   Good quality ingredients produce good compost.

2   You must create a healthy balance between nitrogen and carbon: 1 part nitrogen to 25 parts carbon.

Here is a guide to nitrogen and carbon ingredients:

Carbon matter
- Dry leaves, prunings
- Straw
- Water weeds (rushes)
- Dry grass, paper
- Sawdust (high levels)
- Brassica stalks
- Pine needles
- Wood ash
- Vacuum dust

Nitrogen matter
- Comfrey, yarrow, dandelion
- Poultry and cow manure (high levels)
- Horse manure
- Hair clippings
- Lawn clippings, lucerne, hay
- Seaweed, garden weeds
- Fruit, vegetable peelings
- Pea, bean, tomato haulms
- Tea leaves (low levels)

3   Moisture is important because vital bacteria cannot flourish in dry conditions. Most kitchen scraps and vegetation are 90% water, so will increase the moisture of the compost. The moisture content of the heap should be similar to a lightly squeezed sponge. Moisten all dry ingredients thoroughly. Moist—not wet!

4   Air circulation helps to generate heat and speed up the process.

5   Moist organic materials are heated by the activity of micro-organisms feeding and increasing in number. The composting process is at its most rapid when the temperature range is between 45°C and 55°C.

6   There are two methods of composting: aerobic (a system where the heap is repeatedly aerated by turning or forking) and anaerobic (not turned or forked, thus little or no aeration).

COMPOST HINTS

It is important to place your compost bin in a sheltered sunny position, preferably avoiding the afternoon sun in summer, so as to gain the best results. If this is not possible, your compost may need a little extra attention. Always ensure that your bin has a lid to prevent it from being soaked by rain, and see that the bin is placed on soil for good draining. If a concrete block is the only floor you can offer, sit the bin on a few house bricks or blocks of timber. Using twigs as the bottom layer of the compost heap can also help with drainage.

If you don't have enough organic material to fill your compost bin, half fill the bin and add to it regularly until it is full. Mix nitrogen (vegie scraps) with carbon (leaves, vacuum-cleaner dust) to reduce the risk of problems. When the bin is full, let it stand for 10–16 weeks. It is impossible to maintain the required temperature to make compost in a gradually filled bin, so the process will take longer than if you were to fill the bin all at once.

If you have enough ingredients to fill the bin but little time to spare, add the material in alternate layers of carbon and nitrogen, starting with a carbon layer at the bottom of the bin. When the contents decompose and reduce in size the bin can be topped up.

Repeat this method frequently until the bin reaches full capacity, then let the full bin stand for 10–16 weeks. Here again, the process in being interrupted by gradual filling so it will be slow. If you don't keep filling the bin, then the process will be quicker.

Fast composting

You can have compost for the garden in just 3 or 4 weeks if you have the ingredients to fill the bin and are prepared to aerate it twice a week by lifting the bin off the heap (if it is a plastic bin) and forking through the compost as you return it to the bin. In addition, you may find that a sprinkling of dolomite is required, firstly when you are compiling your heap and then again as it decomposes, to prevent the heap from developing excessive acidity.

Disorders and solutions

Odours

Caused by insufficient air circulation. Rectify by turning the heap with a fork every second day for a week. A wet heap can cause odours too (try adding dry leaves) and excess nitrogen is a another cause—add carbon-based material.

Dry centre

Not enough moisture: add water.

Maggots

Usually found when faeces, seafood, meat and/or fats are amongst the compost materials. Remove the cause, cover the maggots with lime, apply a layer of topsoil to the heap and fork through the next day.

COMPOST RECIPES

Although a recipe is not really necessary some gardeners find security in following tried and tested composting routines. Here are some old and new favourites.

THE 14-DAY COMPOST

1   Finely shred all materials (enough to fill 1 cubic metre)

2   Mix with fine dry manure (chicken, rabbit or sheep manure, or dried cow or horse manure)

3   Toss thoroughly

4   Moisten (don't drench)

5   Turn the heap every 2–3 days to aerate it

6   On the 14th day, add it to the garden

Shredded material is light and fluffy and makes it easy to turn the heap. Over the 14 days the compost undergoes a spectacular colour change—green, grey, silver, brown, blackish brown. The composting process continues after it has been added to the garden and you will find it provides an ideal mulch while breaking down further.

FREE-STANDING COMPOST

This is a heap without a bin.

Note: moisten the layers as you build the heap.

1 The bottom layer consists of rough twigs or small branches

2 Add a layer of green matter (grasses or vegetable scraps)

3 Follow with a light layer of animal manure

4 Dry matter, such as leaves, makes up the next layer

5 Another layer of animal manure

6 More green matter

7 More animal manure

8 Leaves, straw or other dry matter

9 A fine layer of soil or discarded potting mix

10 Animal manure

11 Green matter

12 Cover the whole heap with straw for insulation

Depending on the size of the organic material added (assuming it has not been shredded) the heap may take several months to decay.

STANDARD HEAP

1 Use rough debris for the bottom layer

2 Add a layer of leaves

3 A layer of finely cut grass (no runners)

4 A sprinkling of manure

5 Dampen the pile (don't drench)

6 Add garden refuse, such as shredded prunings, herbs, flowers and vegies

7 Another layer of finely cut grass (again, no runners)

8 Straw, leaves, hair fibres or other dry matter

9 Another sprinkling of manure

10 Add grass cuttings

11 Moisten the heap

This basic recipe is easily adapted for limited ingredients by ensuring that you have a fairly good balance of carbon and nitrogen—check the ingredient guidelines in the previous section. How you choose to use the heap is up to you. You can place it in a plastic commercial bin and let it stand for a few months. You can place it in a bin and fork it every few days. Perhaps you have constructed a three-part compartment bin and will turn it at two stages only. Every keen organic gardener seems to have his or her own super recipe for compost.

⁂ HOME-GROWN INGREDIENTS

The plants in this sample are all rich in nutrients; some are common weeds.

BLACKTHORN (*Prunus spinosa*)
Composted blackthorn leaves help to energise an over-worked soil and revitalise a poor soil.

CHAMOMILE (*Anthemis nobilis, Matricaria chamomilla*)
Rich in calcium, it helps to sweeten the compost heap. Its soothing natural healing and beauty properties and its petite flowers make chamomile a delight in any garden.

CHICKWEED (*Stellaria media*)
Provides a good supply of copper, iron, manganese and potassium. Generally respected in the garden as a quality soil indicator.

COMFREY (*Symphytum officinale, S. asperum, S. grandiflorum*)
Adds calcium, phosphorus, nitrogen and potassium. Highly praised as a compost activator. Grow your comfrey in a large pot and cut its leaves as you need them; the root stock will go on producing more fodder for the compost bin.

DANDELION (*Taraxacum officinale*)
Rich in iron, copper, potassium, sulphur and manganese, it can be found popping up in lawns, cracks in pathways and wherever its nutrients are needed. Earthworms like to travel

along the cavities made by the roots: it often provides them with easy access into a harsh soil so that they can begin their good work. The humble dandelion has the reputation of being the earthworm's friend, as well as an exceptional compost ingredient. It is much loved by bees, too.

Melon
Delicious to eat and that's not all. The leaves of the plant are rich in calcium and will help produce a good quality compost.

SOW THISTLE (*Sonchus oleraceus*)
Rich in iron, potassium, copper, calcium and vitamin C, it seems to grow readily anywhere and everywhere. Its deep roots help to bring nutrients to the surface for other plants to use. Your pet bird or rabbit will want to feast on this nutritious plant. Makes a good ingredient for a home-made liquid plant food as well as the compost heap.

STINGING NETTLE (*Urtica urens, U. dioica, U. incisa*)
Maligned as a weed by some, but adored by organic gardeners because it is outstanding in compost making, as a liquid plant food and as a healing agent for damaged plants. Nettle is well worth growing: it adds iron, copper and calcium, and is recognised as a compost activator. It is advisable to grow this plant in a large container and out of reach of children, however, as it stings readily. Handle with gloves.

TANSY (*Tanacetum vulgare*)
Concentrates lots of potassium and is an asset to any compost heap.

TOMATO (*Lycoperiscon esculentum*)
One of the most popular fruits grown in spring and summer, it thrives on compost made from its fellow tomato plants. Shred some plants and use the 14-day compost system so that it is available for your tomato crops throughout their productive season.

VALERIAN (*Valeriana officinalis*)
Will yield a rich compost when mixed with dandelion, nettle and tansy.

WATERCRESS (*Nasturtium officinale*)
Contains enormous amounts of copper, sulphur and phosphorus. Easily grown in a damp area or pond. A nutritious ingredient for the compost bin!

YARROW (*Achillea millefolium*)
This soft, ferny, low-growing herb with its striking flowers is a super-charged compost ingredient containing copper, nitrates and phosphates. A chopped yarrow leaf placed on each layer of the heap will accelerate the composting process.

PREPARING INGREDIENTS

Finely shredded and prepared ingredients help to speed compost making, so it is advisable to prepare all ingredients before piling them in a heap or a bin.

- **A food processor** can easily prepare kitchen scraps by shredding or mincing them. Herbs can be shredded with the scraps too, or in the following two methods.

- **A lawn mower** will reduce a pile of prunings to splinters in a few minutes. Be careful to wear trousers to protect your legs and glasses to protect your eyes, and avoid flying objects.

- **A shredder** is a wise purchase for those committed to gardening. It turns organic matter to fine shavings. Twigs, discarded timber and garden scraps, once processed, quickly become non-bulky minced materials.

USING COMPOST

There never seems enough compost to do all the jobs you want it to do. Remember, if compost is spread over an area where its nutrients are not picked up almost immediately, the benefits will be largely wasted. Use it where plants are growing, and at their time of maximum growth.

Recognise the needs of your plants, for example that strawberries, asparagus, cauliflowers and celery require a rich soil, which means they will thrive on compost. Plants such as lettuce, spinach, swedes and leeks tolerate a medium quality soil—but that doesn't mean they don't like compost. Plants, like humans, enjoy their favourite foods and prosper from those that give them vitality.

Potting mix
Mix: 2 parts fine compost
     2 parts sphagnum peat
     2 parts sifted soil
     1 part horticultural grit.
Great for cuttings and seedlings.

MULCHING — A RESOURCE FROM GARDEN REFUSE

Many gardeners are aware that they should mulch their garden to retain moisture and suppress weeds, but very few are aware of the full potential of a good mulch. It is not about throwing a few leaves and grass cuttings around the trunk of a tree or raking it on to the garden: companion plants provide nutritional value when applied as mulch. Remember that shredded mulch is preferable because it doesn't block out vital resources such as air and water. Also, think about seasonal conditions. In summer it's best to use light coloured mulches that reflect the light and the heat of the sun, while darker mulches are suitable for winter, as they absorb light and heat.

How can mulch help?

- Mulch conserves moisture in the soil, combatting loss of vitamins due to wilting

- Soil drainage is improved and the soil is conditioned

- Surface crusting is prevented and soil compaction is reduced

- Soil temperatures remain more stable

- It prevents nutrients from being leached out of the soil by the elements

- The management of soil erosion is facilitated

- Crop yields are stimulated

- Frost injury to plants is prevented

- Its odour can deter unwanted insects

- Unwanted weeds are suppressed

- It encourages friends of the garden, such as earthworms and benefical micro-organisms

- Garden waste is recycled

- Mulching saves time in maintaining the garden

Common mulch ingredients

- **Leaves** should be shredded before mulching. They provide a range of nutrients which condition the soil.

- **Grass clippings** are perhaps the most accessible mulch ingredient available to the majority of gardeners. They are rich in nitrogen and break down rapidly. Avoid using any grass clippings that may have been treated with a chemical.

- **Straw** makes a mulch that should be used sparingly with young seedlings. At times it can have a toxic effect.

- **Garden refuse** is a mixture of companion plants and nutritious weeds, so make sure it is free of seeds. So many of the plants can easily re-establish themselves.

Tips for applying mulch

- To suppress weeds, the mulch should be at least ankle deep.

- When applying pine needles to blueberries and strawberries, the mulch should be approximately 75 mm deep.

- ⚘ Shredded leaves and plant matter should be laid in a thin layer.

Companion plants as a living mulch for large shrubs and trees

Bergamot, catmint, catnip, chamomile, chickweed, comfrey, cress, gota kola, lemon balm, lovage, marjoram, moneywort, nasturtium, pennyroyal, salad burnet, soapwort, stinging nettle, yarrow, watercress.

HOME-MADE LIQUID PLANT FOODS

WHY USE A LIQUID PLANT FOOD?

- ⚘ To make nutrients available to plants immediately
- ⚘ To correct deficiencies quickly at fruiting time
- ⚘ To administer first-aid to a damaged plant or garden
- ⚘ To correct deficiencies when transplanting mature plants and seedlings
- ⚘ To provide nutrients for an infertile soil
- ⚘ As fast food for highly productive gardens—that is, fast-maturing and edible gardens

FAST FOOD AND FIRST-AID

Liquid fertiliser makes nutrients available to plants immediately and is taken up within 24 hours, unlike solid fertilisers which can take up to 3 weeks to feed a plant. For fast-maturing plants such as vegetables, a liquid fertiliser provides fast food, keeping pace with their growth and productivity. It offers the same assistance to injured plants and gardens. The appropriate liquid plant food or tonic is taken up immediately, thus reducing plant stress and deterioration.

Making a home-made liquid plant food doesn't require a great deal of time or energy, and is so simple that a child could do it. Unless a plant is large and bulky there is no need to chop up the plant matter beforehand. The whole process of making plant food would take no more than a few moments.

Applying liquid plant food

The rule of thumb in using liquid plant foods and tonics is to dilute the mixture in accordance with the recipe. The dilution assures you of an ample supply and avoids scorching the plants—killing them with kindness. Some plant food mixtures can be made within 3 or 4 days and do not require thinning. Always check the recipe.

Odours and sealed covers

You will notice that the recipes contained in this booklet suggest you brew plant food in a container with a cover or well-fitted lid. Odours accompany most liquid plants foods as they ferment but when the mix matures, odours dwindle to almost nothing. The cover or lid plays a vital role. Not only does it keep odours locked in, it prevents rain from diluting the mix and pests from invading.

Inexpensive utensils and equipment

Just as it takes little skill to make liquid plant food, it also takes a minute amount of equipment:

❀ A plastic garbage bin with fitted lid is a good-sized container for the average garden.

❀ Nappy buckets (with lid) are ideal for the keen gardener who wants a selection of plant foods and tonics available at all times.

❀ The old 44-gallon drum cannot be overlooked either.

❀ A scoop with a long handle is an appropriate serving device. You will appreciate the length of the handle if the mix smells foul. An old tin (sized to suit) fastened securely to the end of a tomato stake or broom handle works well.

 # RECIPES

COMFREY

Comfrey is a popular herb because of its varied role in the garden. It grows easily; if you have a small garden keep comfrey in a large pot as it has invasive habits.

The super mix

- Half fill a container with comfrey leaves. If using a small container you may need to chop the leaves slightly
- Add water, filling the container to the brim
- Seal with a lid or secure cover. Stand in a semi-shaded area
- Allow the mixture to stand for approximately 3 weeks
- Dilute on usage: 50% mixture to 50% water

Apply the fertiliser every 3 weeks during the most vigorous period of growth and production. The mixture is suitable for potted plants, but you will need to dilute it: 20% mixture to 80% water. Apply regularly.

STINGING NETTLE

Don't be frightened of this wonder weed. It won't sting you if you are cautious when handling it—wear thick garden gloves. You'll be pleased you learnt to accept this much-maligned weed. Nettle has more iron than any other land plant. Its value to the garden bed, the compost bin, the treatment of tree wounds and the treatment of ailing plants is exceptional. Keep it in a large pot and don't let it go fully to seed, or it will be everywhere.

The versatile mix

- Pack a container half to three-quarters full of the whole nettle plant. If using a small container chop the plants slightly to make packing easier

- Fill the container to the brim with water (rainwater if possible)

- Allow to stand in a shaded area for approximately 1 week

- Dilute on usage: 1 part mixture to 10 parts water

Use regularly during spring and summer—vegetable plants love it. If you want to use it immediately, let it stand for 3 days and apply without diluting.

Nettle liquid fertiliser is easily adapted for other uses:

Aphid spray

- Dilute fertiliser: 1 part mixture to 20 parts water

- Mix with some pure soap flakes (the soap acts as a fixative). Be careful, too much soap makes the mix turn thick.

- Place in a recycled pump-pack spray

Use for aphid control in the garden. It stores well, but shake it before use.

Plant-wound treatment

Scoop out the plant sludge at the bottom of your nettle fertiliser bin and squeeze out the excess water—you may want to wear waterproof gloves while doing this. Paint the sludge on to a tree or plant wound and watch it heal quickly.

DANDELION

An excellent tonic for potted herbs. In particular, it helps rejuvenate your pot plants on your return from holidays.

The container-plant mix

- ❧ Search your lawn and garden for dandelions
- ❧ Pick them, shake off the soil residue and half fill a bucket with them
- ❧ Add water until the bucket is full
- ❧ Put a cover or lid on the bucket
- ❧ Stand the mix out of direct sunlight for 3 weeks
- ❧ Dilute: 50% mix to 50% water and apply to pot plants when needed

YARROW

Useful as a first-aid plant. Yarrow has long been respected as a nursing plant in companion planting, enhancing the health of neighbouring plants.

The nursing mix

- ❧ Remove any residual soil from the plant(s)
- ❧ Half fill a bucket with yarrow and cover with water

◊ Stand in a shaded area for approximately 3 weeks

◊ Dilute: 40% mix to 60% water

HORSETAIL

A hardy perennial, native to Europe, its history dates back to the earliest ages. It grows from a rhizome and has needle-like stems which reach a height of 30–60 cm. The surface of the stem is thickly coated with silica, hence its reputation as a wonderful medicinal plant. It also contains calcium, cobalt and other minerals, making it an effective treatment for fungal diseases. A liquid fertiliser made from this plant helps to keep your garden healthy.

The perennial mix
◊ Add 2 handfuls equisetum to 18 L water

◊ Boil for half an hour

◊ Let stand for several weeks in a semi-shaded area

◊ Strain and spray

Pest-deterrent paint
Equisetum liquid fertiliser can easily be made into an effective paint for fruit trees, protecting them against insects, eggs and spores.

◊ Take: 3 L horsetail liquid fertiliser
                2 kg clay
                1 kg cow manure

◊ Mix thoroughly

❀ Using a thick brush, apply the paint to the trunk and lower limbs of fruit trees at the end of winter or before budding

Fungal spray

❀ Mix: 40 g fresh horsetail plant (20 g dried plant)
4 L water and a little mild soap
for adhesion

❀ Boil for 20 minutes
❀ Cool, strain and spray

Use this spray at the first sign of plant wilt or mildew.

BLENDED PLANT MIXTURES

Red spider and aphid spray

An effective way of combating red spider and aphids.

❀ Mix: $^1/_2$ cup fresh horsetail ($^1/_4$ cup dried plant)
1 cup stinging nettle leaves
1 L water
a little mild soap for adhesion

❀ Boil for 20 minutes
❀ Cool, strain and spray

The exhausted plant mix

This fertiliser gives a boost to tired plants.

❀ Make horse manure fertiliser: fill a bin with a 50–50 mix of manure and water, then let it stand for 3 weeks

- ◊ Take 1 cup horse manure fertiliser (undiluted)
- ◊ Add 2 cups each nettle, plantain, sage, yarrow, dandelion and chamomile
- ◊ Add 22 L water (rainwater if possible)
- ◊ Stand directly in the sun for 2–3 days
- ◊ Strain and apply the fertiliser directly onto the garden

Tomato booster fertiliser

You will quickly notice the difference in tomatoes when this fertiliser is applied.

- ◊ Half fill a bucket with chopped tomato plant and comfrey
- ◊ Top up with water
- ◊ Stand mixture in a sheltered area for approximately 3 weeks
- ◊ Dilute: 50% mix to 50% water

Apply to fruit-producing tomato plants and watch them burst with renewed vitality. Note: a liquid made only of comfrey will enhance tomato plants during their fruiting period.

General-purpose garden tonic

Suitable for edible, ornamental, and container gardens. This mixture is made in accordance with the needs of your garden or plant(s)—refer to plant nutrient table—using whatever is available: dandelion, chamomile, bracken, tansy, nettle, etc. Mix together plants that will help rectify particular problems in the plants or soil. It makes a good general garden tonic too.

- Half fill a bucket with plant matter

- Top up bucket with water and seal

- Stand it in a sheltered position for approximately 2 weeks

- Dilute: 50% mix to 50% water

NATURAL PLANT FOOD

Plants require a variety of nutrients for their health and well-being. You need look no further than nature, as it provides its own vital food source. It is helpful to know the specific contribution of each nutrient and which plants can provide them. In a well-designed companion-planted garden, natural plant food is abundant and can be made available to plants through liquid fertiliser, compost and mulch.

CALCIUM
Cements cell walls and is vital for the storage of quantities of fruit.

Plants: chives, chamomile, dandelion, meadowsweet, nettle, comfrey, sow thistle, fat hen, horsetail, watercress, burdock, liquorice, Scotch broom.

COBALT
Part of vitamin B for plant healing and general well-being, as well as being essential for the production of nitrogen in legumes.

Plants:

cabbage, cauliflower leaves,
peach tree wastes, legumes.

COPPER

For vitamin C and the production of seeds.

Plants:

yarrow, dandelion, nettle, sow thistle,
watercress, spinach, tobacco.

IRON

One of the components necessary for the formation of green pigment; high levels of potassium are also needed.

Plants:

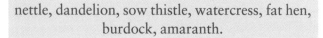

nettle, dandelion, sow thistle, watercress, fat hen,
burdock, amaranth.

MAGNESIUM

Another essential part of green pigment, and is required in germination.

Plants:

peppermint, dandelion, parsley.

MANGANESE

Increases the plant's efficiency and productivity in overcast weather.

Plants:

alfalfa, carrot tops, dandelion, amaranth.

MOLYBDENUM

Increases seeds in pea and bean crops, and helps to manufacture vitamin C.

 Plants: horsetail, alfalfa, ragweed, poplar leaves, peach tree clippings, corn stalks.

NICKEL
Involved in the production of certain vitamins.

 Plants: buckwheat, peas and beans.

NITROGEN
Needed by all cells for reproduction and growth; increases the yields of fruit and leaf vegetables.

Plants: nettle, comfrey, dandelion, apple leaves, clover, soy bean, alfalfa, bracken.

PHOSPHORUS
Stimulates early root formation and growth. It is particularly important to root crops.

Plants:
sorrel, garlic, caraway, calendula, nettle, dandelion, fat hen, liquorice.

POTASSIUM
Helps plants to utilise nitrogen and improves the flavour and keeping quality of fruit and vegetables. It helps to make healthy pollen and is essential to fruit trees.

Plants:
borage, chamomile, mint, nettle, summer savory, cress, tansy, comfrey, dandelion, sow thistle, watercress, sunflower, evening primrose.

SULPHUR
Increases root growth and helps to manufacture B vitamins.

Plants:
dandelion, watercress.

ZINC
Transforms carbohydrates and regulates the intake of sugars in plants.

Plants:
corn stalks, alfalfa, peach tree wastes.

✿ LET YOUR GARDEN LOOK AFTER YOU

FAVOURITE SWEET POTPOURRI RECIPES

Drying herbs

To dry the herbs I usually place them in a stocking and hang it in a tree for around 2 weeks. Occasionally I give it a shake. When the mix has dried, I toss it thoroughly with orris root powder to fix the scent. To reduce large leaves to a fine ingredient, I simply rub them in the palm of my hand.

Suitable flower petals

Calendula, candytuft, carnations, chamomile (Roman), delphinium, forget-me-not, heliotrope, honeysuckle, hyacinth, jasmine, lavender, lilac, lily of the valley, mignonette, orange blossoms, peony, roses, violets and wallflowers.

Suitable leaves

Basil, bay, eucalyptus, geranium (scented), lemon balm, lemon verbena, lovage, marjoram, mints, myrtle, rosemary, sage, southernwood, sweet germander, sweet woodruff, tarragon, thyme and wormwood.

Cottage garden fragrance potpourri

Mix together 1 cup of each of the following dry ingredients:

- sweet basil
- rosemary
- sweet marjoram
- lemon balm
- thyme

Astringent air freshener

Mix:

- ¹/₂ cup mint
- 1 cup basil
- 1 cup rosemary leaves
- 1 cup lemon thyme leaves
- 2 cups crushed lemon verbena leaves

Toss well

HERBAL BATHS

A herbal bath can cause a magical, uplifting or deeply thera-peutic effect. Selected herbs can relax the body, stimulate circulation or rejuvenate tired muscles. And the aroma of highly fragrant herbs can linger for an hour, creating a feel-ing of spring in your home.

HERBAL BATHING

Make a draw-string bag out of muslin or fine gauze (12 cm x 8 cm). Fill it with an appropriate herb—or several. Hang it over the hot tap and allow the water to flow through it as the bath is filling. Ensure that the water is warm, not hot. If the body heats rapidly you will perspire, preventing the skin from absorbing the properties of the herbs. Enjoy the bath; lay back and relax for 10–15 minutes.

Healing herbs: calendula, comfrey, houseleek, lady's mantle, spearmint, yarrow.
Relaxing herbs: chamomile, jasmine, lime flowers, meadowsweet, valerian.

Rejuvenating herbs: basil, bay, fennel, lavender, lemon balm, lemon verbena, mint, pennyroyal, rosemary, sage, tansy, thyme.

FLOWER ARRANGEMENTS

The companion-planted garden offers an array of flowers and foliage to enhance the decor of the home. Whether fresh or dried, their combined aroma removes stale odours, leaving a lingering scent of the garden.

Use new and fresh plants to guarantee the longevity of the flower arrangement. Avoid using flowers which are bruised or have petals missing as they will wilt rapidly. Check leaves for signs of withering.

Equipment

To avoid the disease and bruising which can occur during harvesting and arranging, you will need well-maintained scissors and secateurs to make a clean, smooth cut. For really thick and tough branches use long-handled secateurs.

Flowers

Angelica, bergamot, borage, chamomile, chicory, columbine, cornflower, cowslip, dill, elecampane, feijoa, forget-me-not, foxglove, herb Robert, honeysuckle, jasmine, lady's mantle, larkspur, lavender, lily of the valley, love-in-a-mist, marigold, marjoram, meadowsweet, melilot, mints, mock orange, nasturtium, primrose, pyrethrum, rose, rosemary, thymes, valerian, violet, wallflower, yarrow.

Foliage

Ajuga, artemisia, basil, bay, buxus, chervil, curry plant, elderberry, feijoa, fennel, lemon balm, lemon verbena, lungwort, marjoram, mint, mullein, parsley, geraniums, rosemary, sage, salad burnet, santolina, sweet germander, thymes.

Further information

Earthkeepers gardens are open to the public on selected days during spring and summer. From time to time, field days are held.

Contact:
Earthkeepers (Note: now located in Young, NSW)
PO Box 1466
Young NSW 2594

www.earthkeepers.com.au

Recommended reading

Catton, Chris and Gray, James *The Incredible Heap: A Guide to Compost Gardening*, St. Martin's Press, 1983.

Creasy, Rosalind, *The Complete Book of Edible Landscaping*, Sierra Club, 1982.

Goodwin, Jill, *A Dyer's Manual*, Pelham Books Ltd, 1982.

Gordon, Lesley and Lorimer, Jean, *The Complete Guide to Drying and Preserving Flowers*, Chartwell Books, 1982.

Hawken, Paul, *The Magic of Findhorn*, Fontana, 1976.

Kourik, Robert, *Designing and Maintaining Your Edible Landscape Naturally*, Metamorphic Press, 1986.

Mollison, Bill, *Introduction to Permaculture*, Tagari Publications, 1991.

Morrow, Rosemary, *Earth User's Guide to Permaculture*, Kangaroo Press, 1993.

Piercy, Harold, *The Constance Spry Handbook of Floristry*, Christopher Helm, 1984.

Squire, David, *The Scented Garden*, Doubleday, 1989.

Index

barberry 66

basil 62, 63, 66, 88, 104, 108, 114, 116, 147, 148, 149, 150

bay 67, 147, 149, 150

bean beetle 47, 49, 110

beans 47, 80, 82, 86, 87, 91, 92, 99, 101, 105, 108, 111, 116, 144, 145

beans, broad 57, 67, 76, 100, 105

beans, bush or snap 62, 67, 74, 79, 113

beans, lima 67

beans, runner 67, 68, 74

bees 57, 68, 69, 73, 77, 78, 79, 83, 91, 97, 128

beetroot 68, 92, 94, 110, 111

Berberis darwinii 66

   B. vulgaris 66

bergamot 68, 134, 149

Beta vulgaris 68

   B. vulgaris var. *cicla* 111

black alder 69

blackberry 107

blackcurrant (*see* currant)

blackthorn 127

blueberry 69, 81, 104, 133

bombardier beetle 51, 52

borage 44, 45, 47, 60, 69, 111, 113, 146, 149

Borago officinalis 69

borers 47, 49, 76, 79

box (*see* buxus)

bracken 48, 53, 69, 87, 142, 145

braconid wasp 52

bramble berries 115

Brassica alba 98

   B. campestris oleifera 106

   B. campestris var. *rapa* 116

   B. chinensis 76

B. naprobrassica 114

B. napus 106

B. oleracea 69, 77

B. oleracea var. *bulata gemmifera* 70

B. oleracea acephala 91

B. oleracea caulorapa 92

B. oleracea var. *botrytis* 73

B. oleracea var. *capitata* 70

broccoli 69, 100

bronchial relief 61

brown rot 85

bruising, relief of 71, 105

brussels sprout 16, 70

buckwheat 57, 145

bud mite 72

burdock 55, 143, 144

bush melon 79

bush squash 79

buxus 70, 150

Buxus sempervirens 70

cabbage 14, 70, 72, 76, 79, 93, 97, 99, 100, 102, 103, 108, 110, 115, 144

cabbage butterfly 49, 70, 91, 100

cabbage worm 14, 61, 70, 115

calamint 64, 71, 86

Calamintha officinalis 71

calcium 55, 56, 81, 88, 110, 118, 127, 128, 129, 140, 143

calendula 71, 74, 85, 93, 110, 146, 147, 148

Calendula officinalis 71

camellia 72, 86

Camellia japonica 72

   C. reticulata 72

   C. sasanqua 72

candytuft 48, 72, 147

canola 106

Cape gooseberry 72, 87

capsicum (*see* peppers) 63, 66, 71

Capsicum frutescens var. *grossum* 104

   C. frutescens var. *fasiculatum* 103

   C. frutescens var. *longum* 103

caraway 72, 146

carbon in compost 120, 121, 122, 123, 126

Carica papaya 101

carob 72, 73, 93

carotene 55

carnation 147

carrot 16, 64, 68, 73, 82, 93, 99, 100, 101, 108, 109, 110

carrot fly 49, 109

Carum carvi 72

Carya illinoinensis 102

Castanea sativa 75

caterpillar 52, 82, 88

catmint 58, 60, 64, 66, 68, 72, 73, 75, 84, 87, 88, 89, 92, 94, 95, 100, 102, 104, 111, 112, 134

catnip 44, 48, 59, 60, 62, 72, 73, 75, 76, 89, 91, 104, 105, 134

cats 64, 73

cauliflower 16, 68, 73, 75, 76, 79, 102, 119, 131, 144

Cedronella canariensis 64

celeriac 74, 93

celery 51, 67, 69, 74, 93, 131

Centaurea cyanus 79

Ceratonia siliqua 72

chalcid wasp 52